(blue)

FINAL THOUGHTS

INSIDE & OUTSIDE THE BOX

JACK IDLE

Grosvenor House
Publishing Limited

The right of Jack Idle to be identified as the author of this
work has been asserted in accordance with Section 78
of the Copyright, Designs and Patents Act 1988

The book cover is copyright to Jack Idle

This book is published by
Grosvenor House Publishing Ltd
Link House
140 The Broadway, Tolworth, Surrey, KT6 7HT.
www.grosvenorhousepublishing.co.uk

A CIP record for this book
is available from the British Library

ISBN 978-1-83975-193-6

THE BLACK EDITION

$\dfrac{52}{200}$

CONTENTS

INTRODUCTION

This book is the third I have dedicated to my old friend Jack Ware (1931-2019), and to all those who lost their lives in failed attempts to escape reality.

It was only half written when Jack, still clinging to his now empty bucket, finally let go. It rolled across his bedroom floor, in that drunken haphazard way that buckets do, and Jack appeared to wave goodbye to it as it crossed the threshold into the next room. And with that, he took his knowledge and memories with him into the future to entertain new audiences.

Once more it is a mix of stuff that crossed my desktop, or popped into or out of my head, out of the blue, and inspired me to divert my energies away from more serious matters. Since it is the final book in the trilogy, it has drifted into black humour, some of which is very black indeed, focused on the darker and more serious of human obsessions. And it includes even more self-indulgent, biographical events and other stuff, but hopefully interesting or familiar enough to raise a sad and knowing smile or two. Some of the content is a grim reflection on humanity and the state of the world today, and the direction we are heading, with little if any hope of avoiding self-destruction.

If you have been foolish or unlucky enough to have acquired this load of nonsense, or you are as depressed as I have become lately with global stupidity, do not attempt to read more than a couple of pages at a sitting, unless you are under sedation, suffer from insomnia, or you have run out of paper…

———————

PROLOGUE

Does Jack Idle exist, or is he a figment of your imagination, or his own? And would he know the answers, or care? Whatever they are, this book is unlikely to shed any light on them.

What is known is that his name is real, given to him by his stepfather, but otherwise he has become his own fictional character, and a master of reinvention.

The reality is that none of the characters named or described in the following pages are real people, and any similarity with a real person of the same name is entirely coincidental, unless they aren't real either.

Any opinions expressed by any of the characters named or depicted in the book are entirely their own, or borrowed from other fictional characters, and are not necessarily those of the author, although they might be.

And almost none of the events referred to or described in the book ever happened, at least not yet, unless there is a double negative in there somewhere. In which case they probably did, and may be an alternative history that has yet to be written, if it hasn't been done so already.

None of this really matters. And if you have already lost interest or the plot, or the page-count to see how much is left before you can claim to have read the book, you might want to take out your crayons, and simply colour in all the 'o's, for example, and turn the book into a visual work of art, then count those instead, which you may find more entertaining, or at least therapeutic.

———————

There are some things so serious you have to laugh at them.

Niels Bohr

Hello, my name is Idle, Jack Idle. My friends call me Jack, but you can call me 'Sir'.

I know lots of famous people, most of them dead.

Ron: I haven't seen you in such a long time, I thought you must be dead.
Jack: Me too, if they catch me, or you.

Jack: I thought I saw you last week at your service?
Ron: No, that was me at yours.

I never knew he had so many friends, until they turned up at his wake with their empty glasses.

The difference between flirting and harassment is often only a financial one.

Another is the physical appeal of the alleged culprit. Flirting if he's a handsome hunk, and harassment if he's an ugly jerk.

I was such an ugly baby, mother used to pull my pram.

Gott upphaf gerir góðan endi.

(Icelandic proverb)*

PUB TALK 1

He: Where are you from, my dear, and what can I get you?

She: Alava large G 'n' T, without the T, and Liverpoool, luv. Wydjer wanna know?

He: You must have quite a bit of the Irish in you then?

She: Not anymore, luv, never since that last one did a runner before I'd even 'ad chance to pullup me drawers.

_____

She: Okay, so what's your excuse for coming home at this hour, again?

He: Sorry, dear, but there was a knock-out competition at the pub, to see who had the best wife, and I know you aren't going to believe this, but I won...

_____

When God gave man his first multi-tool, He was obviously having an off-day, or it was April 1st.

_____

As I undressed for bed and surveyed my bruised and aching body, from black eye and broken nose to crushed ribs and painful groin, I remembered that once again she had got out of bed on the wrong side this morning.

_____

Never let sex get in the way of a perfect friendship.

_____

In these depressing times with idiots on both sides of the Atlantic, we need some capable women in charge, if only to keep our peckers up.

After a blazing row, the wife packed my bags and told me to leave. As I walked out of the door, she shouted,

"And I hope you have a slow, painful death."

I said, "Does that mean you now want me to stay?"

I should have seen the signs that things had cooled down when she stopped ironing my socks.

HOLY SOCKS

My conversion to the Pope's sock maker, Gammarelli, proved to be a religious blessing when I discovered they had miraculously cured my holey shoes.

PASSENGER SAFETY FIRST

Airplane seat belts keep you strapped in, solely to help investigators identify your remains after the plane crashes.

Cruise ship lifebelts are provided to allow desperate passengers to escape their boring fellow 'cruisers'.

(A good beginning makes a good ending.)

LESSONS FROM SUBTOPIA

Liverpool is famous for its world pioneering, city-wide sewer system, but it has much more to teach the world about public convenience and town planning:

- The General Hospital is next to the cemetery.
- Recycling was invented when it was observed that the same bunches of flowers often travelled in both directions.
- The UK's first pedestrianised street joined the Maternity Hospital and the Registry Office, with dedicated footways in each direction. Since 1946 the record still stands at 19.45 seconds.
- The City Courts are located on the main shoplifting street.
- Liverpool pioneered home delivery services to include your shoplifting.
- Charity shops will accept anything, with or without price tags.
- The city centre primary school is within frog-marching distance of the Juvenile Court.
- Police Stations are located adjacent to or opposite off-licences.
- All off-licences offer 24/7 emergency deliveries and accept benefit orders as ID and proof of credit worthiness.
- Benefit orders are accepted as legal tender.
- Council tenancy agreements are tradable assets.
- Every car park includes a car accessory and wheel replacement shop.
- Liverpool residents pioneered the UK's first car sharing scheme, by leaving their cars unlocked.

CONFUSED

Following a recent crime incident in the street, and the Metropolitan Police mixing up of our addresses, the Royal Mail delivers my mail to my neighbour's house, four doors away, and vice versa. They probably believe she and I are now co-habiting in both properties, or as two geriatrics, neither of us now able to remember which property we actually live in.

———

As a criminal mastermind, he found his double-digit IQ was more than enough to outsmart the police.

———

I've bought myself a smart new analogue watch that is clear, clever and simple. I know it's lunchtime when both hands point up to the sky, and bedtime when they point at the mouse's feet.

———

RHETORICAL QUESTIONS

- Does my bum look big in this?
- Is the Pope a Catholic?
- You aren't still in the pub, are you?
- Do I look stupid?
- Was that a rhetorical question?

———

Even my mother noticed that since the advent of feminism, there are many more women rising to public prominence, mainly due to them being women, mostly with attitude and long hair cascading down their chests.

———

1511951-5
IDLE, J.
Liverpool City Police

FIRST OFFICIAL PHOTOGRAPH

28 October 2011 10:54 am

Dear Jack and Trish

Greetings from Civilisation.

Despite promising never to put ourselves into the clutches of the US TSA, we have come up with a cunning privacy-defence plan, so that we can again make our annual pilgrimage to the Sunshine State this November. Resplendent in our X-ray proof, depleted-uranium-coated underwear, we will be heading for NPB on the 28th, and thence to Miami on the 29th.

Are you in town and able to receive two radiant guests? If not, catch our exploits in the *Palm Beach Post.*

Tony and Jean

———

October 28, 2011 5:17 pm

Dear Tony and Jean

Greetings from Paradise.

We would be delighted to receive two radiant guests. How about arriving at least a couple of days prior to your descent into that den of iniquity known as Miami?

We are fully recovered from last year's trip there, and from our August / September campaign through nine countries centred on the Baltic states. We easily got into Leningrad and couldn't see why the Germans did not.

They probably failed to tip everyone sufficiently at the border crossing.
All for now, and we look forward to seeing you soon.

Jack + Trish

———

29 October 2011 4:19 pm

Dear Jack and Trish

Thank you for the invitation. We have a tight itinerary but can and will cut short part of it to be with you the day before, Sunday 27th sometime in the afternoon, assuming our undies have dropped to a safe level, of radiation, that is.

Tony and Jean

———

October 29, 2011 11:40 am

Dear Jean and Tony,

We are delighted you can stay two nights with us, arriving Sunday 27th November in the afternoon.
As Jack says, if you find that doesn't work well for you after all and you can only manage one night, we'll grin and bear it. Just let us know if there is a change when you're on the west coast, and you can wash your undies here.

Jack +Trish

———

AMAZON REVIEW 1

The Pound Coin Holder

Better than my money belt and easier to access.

I just love this gadget. I was so excited about solving my loose change nightmare, that I ordered mine Express-Overnight delivery. I liked it so much I ordered two of them, so that I can slip one into each pocket of my skinny Gucci's without spoiling their lines. I really hate seeing those rough guys with bulging pockets, rattling as they strut around. And I can carry a whole £10 without looking like a high roller, which I am most definitely not.

Jack

My wife's excellent homemade biscuits are always generously offered to her afternoon tea guests with,

"Do help yourselves; the first one is free…"

He: Where are we going to be on the 12th February?
She: Well, it's very close to our anniversary, so probably in the same place.
He: That answer doesn't really help me, and…
She: It's the 14th, and surely after 50 years you remember that date?

To quote the oft quoted Paul Dirac, "Yes."

NOSTALGIA 1

Tony and I went to different schools together. Tony's school was posher than mine because it had more Jewish boys. He would often get on the same bus as them, rather than wait for the next one. But they were mostly swots and sat upstairs, closer to God, while Tony and his mate, Wishy-Washy, the son of the Chinese laundry owner, sat downstairs and mucked around with Biffo, Slug, Snig and Yiddy, who wasn't a swot, and would kick a ball around with Golly and Sambo and the 'black-hand gang', who had arrived in Liverpool from the Caribbean on the banana boats. Such happy innocent times, well at least until they were all kicked off the bus.

———

In a society that is now regularly compelled to reinterpret and twist anyone's words or thoughts into 'offensive language', it would be sensible if all politicians and other opinionated people in the public eye were seen and never heard, like children in a bygone age.

———

Come to think of it, BJ is the only one I have never heard apologise for any of his lies, misdeeds, stupidity, offensive insults, or his incoherence.

———

General Elections are a waste of time; the government always gets in.

———

"The authority of a thousand is not worth the humble reasoning of a single individual."

———

LETTER TO FT

Sir

LONDON'S ZERO ROAD DEATHS UTOPIA

Surprisingly, precise official numbers are not easily obtained, but a Google Maps webpage presented under the banner of Vision Zero, the international road safety lobby, clearly flags up site locations and therefore numbers that undermine the claims of a larger problem. According to this map, pedestrian fatalities within London's Congestion Charge Zone (CCZ) in 2017, 2018, and 2019 were 5, 1, and 4, respectively.

In the Mayor and TfL's admirable drive to reduce those already very small numbers down to an unachievable 'zero road deaths', the CCZ speed limit is to be reduced from 30mph to 20mph, despite neither speed ever having been previously achieved anywhere within the CCZ for more than a few seconds at a time, due to traffic congestion and other factors.

The simple, unarguable mathematical consequence of this new, misdirected and counter-productive traffic management intervention will be a further reduction in the 7.4mph current average traffic speed, resulting in yet more traffic congestion, and despite the absurd counter claims, more poisonous pollution, and millions more man-hours lost in 'zero productivity'.

If the saving of lives is of paramount importance to our political servants, regardless of the financial and health penalties, we may soon expect a national speed limit down to a 'safe' 4mph walking pace, with any moving vehicle preceded by a flag carrying safety marshal.

Jack Idle

————

Alternatively, we could close central London to all traffic, including e-bikes and e-scooters, and turn it into a danger-free pedestrian zone. Or even more ridiculously, why not save more lives by extending the new regime to the whole country. Or better still, let's have a national 'lockdown'.

————

Since on average around 20,000 people die each year in UK from flu, compared with 456 pedestrians in 2018, our taxes may be better spent on boosting the NHS rather than changing road signs from 30 to 20mph

————

In all spheres of life, and especially in politics, many men flatter themselves as being born natural leaders, even though they rely on their wives to organise their lives for them and to tell them what to do.

However, all women have proven leadership abilities, especially in leading men astray.

————

She: Stiffen your resolve, Jack, this is not the time to go wobbly on me.

————

Opportunity came knocking, but I couldn't be arsed...

————

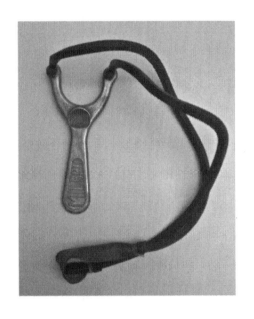

EXHIBIT A

Regina v Idle

JACK AND THE BEANSTALK
or just another tall story

I was born into a working-class family in post-war Liverpool where I had quite a tough childhood. The key to my survival and 'street-cred' was my first catapult, subsequently confiscated by my wicked stepfather after I broke a pane of glass in a neighbour's greenhouse.

He reported me to the police, and as a result, I was sent to an approved school for naughty boys, where they pinned my ears back and tied my thumbs together, just for fun, and where I had to sleep with my football boots on in case the other boys stole them. The school was so tough it had its own coroner.

After my release, I returned home, a caravan on bricks, to find that the locks had been changed, bars put on the windows, and my parents had gone travelling in search of a new set of wheels. However, I was able to pick the lock on the coal-shed door, where I survived on coal nuggets, garden worms and library books until they returned a few months later with five more children. We were so poor some of them didn't even have names, and so poor we had to save the food on our plates for the next meal, or the one after that. After my grandfather died, the number of children grew to match the increased supply of old shoes, but no more names.

At the age of eleven, I was sent to Quarry Bank for a six-year term, a notorious school that as its name implies, trained its inmates in the skills of 'breaking and entering'. Here, I applied myself wholeheartedly to metalwork and made a set of lock-picks for future use, and a catapult which I still sleep with under my pillow.

The skills I picked up were confidence-boosting, but I was never really settled, because I was unsure why my stepfather packed me off at weekends with a week's worth of stale crusts and a demagnetised compass all wrapped up in an old map of Albion. Fortunately, I always managed to find them, wherever they had moved the caravan.

After completing four years of my sentence at 'Quarry', my stepfather tried to get me out on parole. Disguised as generosity towards me, his selfish financial aim was to enrol me as an apprentice to the local chimney sweep, but Governor Pobjoy sent him packing, ensuring that I would serve the full term.

After my stepfather abandoned us, taking the caravan with him, we were much happier, even though we had to take turns sleeping in the single bed in the coal shed. We were so poor, I only had one wheel on my bicycle, and one channel on the black and white TV set that we had 'borrowed' from the neighbours.

Despite the hardships, for my 16th birthday my mother knitted me my first long trousers and socks, 'all-in-ones', and extended my football boots to cover my toes. This boosted my confidence further, to the extent that I was able to leave home, change my name, and to get a lowly paid job on a local building site, starting at the bottom of the ladder.

After several weeks of drain-laying, I realised I disliked the middle-class toffs looking down on me in the trench, and that I needed to raise my sights. So, I stuck a pencil behind my ear, donned a bow tie and signed up as an architectural student at the local College of Building.

Once there, I acquired those essential middle-class badges – drinking wine instead of beer, swapped my Biro for a fountain pen and bought a duvet, and really started my ascent up the social ladder. As I neared the top, I was able to look down loftily on the middle-class bosses, criticise their incompetence, and wallow in superiority in my ivory tower.

During forty years of masquerading as an architect and town planner, I learned the art of 'talki-tecture' and avoided the crime of building anything that would qualify as 'archi-torture'. During that period, I amassed a small fortune, but large enough to allow me to move out of subtopia and indulge in swanky foreign cars, designer-labelled togs, and expensive wallpaper, and so complete the escape from my working-class roots.

In the self-satisfied smugness that characterises the upwardly mobile, my last remaining ambition had been a solo ascent of Everest from where I planned to conduct mankind in an anthem to myself. Then I thought, 'I can't be arsed, I'll send them a selfie and text instead…'

My wife says all I think about is sex, sex, and sex. She's right, of course, three times in fifty years.

She wiped the floor with me after I got home drunk again last night, and it wasn't on the shag-pile.

I wonder if clouds ever look down at me and think, "What's that idiot staring at?"

NOSTALGIA 2

I remember when I was thirteen years old asking my best friend, Yiddy, if I could become Jewish and bunk off school assembly like him.
He said I was mad, and even though God was Jewish he was thinking of swapping sides, like Jesus, especially after what they'd done to his willy without even asking him.

I bought a new electric toothbrush today, and was mystified by the page-full of instructions and safety advice that included:

- Do not use unapproved attachments.
- Do not swallow.
- If swallowed seek medical advice.
- Keep away from children.

FINAL COUNTDOWN

Dr A: Good morning, Mr Idle, what can I do for you?
Me: I think I'm suffering from a terminal illness.
Dr A: Oh dear, what are the symptoms?
Me: Well, I'm now seventy three and three quarters…

Free speech is for all, whether you or they like it, or not.

I love winning prizes, even booby prizes if they're the nice wobbly variety.

There are very few disagreements that can't be resolved with a stick of dynamite.

————

I always try to set an example to others, even if it's just a warning to them.

————————

SIZE MATTERS

She: Is it true you can now buy extra-large condoms?
Pharmacist: It certainly is, Miss. Nowadays, we have more and more regular customers for them.
She: Really, and would you mind if I sit down a while, just to see who they are, and where they hang out?

————————

PC MADNESS

Canadian Prime Minister Justin Trudeau's vilification for his 'racist behaviour', when as a student he 'blacked up' for a fancy-dress party, has now been followed by another but unrelated witch-hunt gaining momentum – the rounding up and defrocking of those awful pantomime dames.

————

Any white man who even thinks of 'blacking up' deserves to be horse-whipped, tarred and feathered, and run out of town.

————————

Once I reached the age of seventy, I no longer felt obliged to conceal my insanity.

————————

ACTIONS SPEAK LOUDER THAN WORDS

A little guy was sat in a café one day eating his lunch, when three tattooed bikers walked in, looked around, and decided to have some fun with him.

They sat down at his table. One took his coffee away from him and drank it. The next one took his sandwich and ate it. The third biker took his apple pie and wolfed that down too.

Without saying a word, the little guy got up, went to the till, paid his bill, and walked out into the carpark.

One of the bikers looked at the waitress, and said, "Did you see that? We took his coffee, his sandwich, and his apple pie and he didn't say a word. He's not much of a man, is he?"

The waitress turned and said, "He's not much of a driver, either. He's just crushed three motorcycles with his truck."

After I won the lottery, I went off on a world cruise, and my wife got her shoes repaired.

Before you throw out your old squeaky shoes, make sure the mice are still at home, and haven't moved on.

When I signed up at my local college on the 'Self Help' course, I was the only one there, not even a tutor.

EXHIBIT B

Regina v Idle

CARE FOR THE ELDERLY?

An old man, not me, went to his doctor and asked the matronly receptionist if he could make an appointment:

Receptionist: Yes, she can see you on the 31st January.

Man: Is that this year or next?

Receptionist: This year.

Man: But that's three weeks away; can't I see her sooner?

Receptionist: Is it an emergency?

Man: No, but it might be in three weeks-time, if I am still alive then.

Receptionist: If you tell me what the problem is, I could look at the appointments diary again for you.

Man: Well, I have a large swelling on my penis, and I can't pass water. It may just be a massive erection, but either way, I think she should have look at it.

Receptionist: Hmm, I see. Well, if you want to come back after surgery, I'll try and fit you in.

Even schoolchildren have now jumped on the climate bandwagon. Fair enough, but are they really willing to give up their phones, computers, TVs, latest trainers, and their lifts to and from school every day?

I went to a gallery preview of Grayson Perry's new work, during which he graciously led his audience through the show, explaining the ideas and imagery in his pots, rug and tapestry.
At the end of the evening I thanked him for his talk, and wished him good luck with the sale of his crockery, and other home furnishings.

———

Date: Wed, Sep 25, 2019 11:38 am

Subject: A Brief Audience with Grayson.

Dear Victoria

Thank you for including me on your list of guests for the gallery preview, and the excellent homemade refreshments afterwards. And please accept my apologies for not taking the early and only opportunity to speak to you at length. However, I did ask your partner to relay my thanks for the splendid evening.

And please pass on to Philippa and Mary my thanks for rescuing me from my isolated corner where I was tucking into your delicious grub, and for their double-act entertainment, not surpassed since two uniformed ladies once pinned me to the floor of *The Flying Dutchman* in Camberwell for several hours.

Thank you again for the memorable evening.

Kind regards

Jack

———

Call me naïve, but it wasn't until I was twenty-three years old that I made the connection between girls and my secondary school biology lessons.

———

I was mystified why my first girlfriend was nicknamed 'Spanner', until she tightened my nuts.

———

If I do get into Heaven, I want a seat on the end of the back row, so I can sneak out if it's boring.

———

PILTDOWN MAN ON THE MOON

Buried remains of *Eoanthropus Dawsoni's* descendants have been discovered at *Mare Tranquillitatis* on the Moon, along with unstamped Apollo XI postcards dated 20th July 1969.

———

After an almighty scream from the bathroom this morning, I rushed in expecting to find another spider in the bath, but this time it was only a grey hair.

Then she said she thought she had seen a new mole on her back, but I couldn't find it, and assumed after her scream it had jumped back out of the window.

———

My girlfriend's DIY skills have come along in leaps and bounds. Not only can she now assemble any piece of flat-pack furniture, but she can disassemble it with a single blow.

———

DIVINE INTERVENTION?

When Jack's son realised that the lady he loved and wanted to marry had misread his reserved nature for indifference and was about to marry her new man in far off Barcelona, he decided to get on his bike and ride the near 1000 miles to propose to her. But it was not to be. He got as far as Basel in Switzerland, where he ended up in hospital for six weeks after he was knocked off his bike when a drunken priest staggered into his path.

———————

Last night, I had a nightmare that I starved to death after my wife had left me, without first making my breakfast.

———————

Every year I buy my wife a new lipstick for her birthday, but none of them have ever worked.

————

I won't make that mistake again, well, not until next time.

———————

This morning on TV I saw dramatic images of the impact of climate change on Minnesota – about five feet of it.

————

All I hear on the radio and television these days is climate change, climate change, climate change.
I blame it on the weathermen.

———————

I am a vehement believer in the democratic process, as long as people vote the way I think.

———————

America is now a nation of men with their wives broadly telling them what not to do and what not to think, but not yet a nation ready to have just one woman telling them all what to do and think.

VISITING TIME

She: You've only been in here three months and the kids are already beginning to ask awkward questions.

He: Well, just tell them I'm on holiday or working abroad, or something…

She: No, they want to know where you stashed the loot.

My scepticism is rooted in the proverbial experience that two in the bushes are better than one in the hand.

MERRY CHRISTMAS

If you want to escape this year's claustrophobia, invite your family to spend Christmas with you, and enjoy the peace, quiet and goodwill by staying at their place.

Happiness is having a large, loving, close-knit family in another city.

If the press can't get their English right, how can anyone be confident their facts are correct?

NINCOMPOOPOLIS

Nincompoopolis is the title of Douglas Murphy's very fair exposé of Boris Johnson's flamboyant but incompetent tenure as Mayor of London, and the follies and scars that his cavalier truncated thinking has left on the city.

Unfortunately, thanks to his 15 million gullible flock, he has been let loose on the whole of a crumbling UK. Depressing and entertaining in equal measure.

Having children should be delayed as long as possible. When you are dependent on pills for your arthritis, blood pressure, depression, and paranoid schizophrenia, you will need them to open the child-proof bottles.

I can get drunk on one drink, usually the thirteenth.

After I'd had one or two drinks too many, again, I joined the AA, thinking that they offered roadside assistance to inebriated drivers.

Has the world gone mad, or is it just me? After the spate of arrests of hotel guests and others for being 'naked or improperly dressed' in the privacy of their own spaces, I make sure I answer the door wearing my posing pouch.

Since the misandry pandemic, sex has become an odds-on Russian Roulette gamble.

MISANDRY
2020
Dan Dare

photo appropriation of *Fenicia* by Mimmo Rotella

BRIEF ENCOUNTERS

Dear Nadine

It was nice to see you again at last night's midnight film screening, and I assume the forgotten package was due to your excitement at the prospect of meeting up again. It has occurred to me that we could use this package as a cover to carry on meeting in the small hours. So let's have another go soon, before my advancing years and memory permanently dampen my enthusiasm for such clandestine goings-on.

Jack

PS. I hope you remembered to put your drawers on this morning?

        ―――

Hi Jack
I will be at the cinema again this Friday, and if we can hook up there, I will give you the goodies then?

Nx

        ―――

Hi Nx

It will be good to get my hands on them at last, but the hook sounds dangerous. Last time I hooked up with a woman, I ended up at her place with her bra.

Jx

―――――――

CLOSE ENCOUNTERS OF THE FIRST AID KIND

Earlier that evening I had been quietly sipping a glass of champagne, and here I was, at midnight, in the local A+E, bloodied, battered, bruised and clothes in tatters.

Doctor: Good God, what happened to you, you look like a stampede hit you?

Me: Well, in a way it was. I was attacked by a bunch of middle-aged women who mistook me for Alan Rickman, and they all wanted a piece of me.

Doctor: But he's dead, isn't he, died a few years ago?

Me: Yes, and that was what I kept telling them as I pleaded for mercy and no scars, but you know what women are like, once they get an idea into their heads, you can talk to them until you are blue in the face, as I am now, and they just don't listen to you…

―――

In reality, I tripped up on a joint and went arse over tit, but fortunately the pavement broke my fall, and unfortunately, my nose and teeth.

―――

As I lay in the gutter bleeding to death, the first person to help me up was a passing paramedic who sat me on a nearby bench. As he was checking me for signs of concussion, a passing doctor offered his assistance too. Both of them advised me to get the no.73 bus to the hospital, rather than wait for an ambulance, which I did. In a way, I suppose, it was my lucky day.

―――

The time between slipping and smacking my face on the pavement was measured in bananoseconds, and the after-effects in megahurts.

She: What do you think of my 'one size fits all' frock?
He: I think you missed the disclaimer – 'But not you'.

My friend Leslie's cross-dressing secret only came to light one night when his hidden wardrobe came crashing through the bedroom ceiling and landed on his wife, who thought Christmas had come early.

He might have got away with it, but none of it was her size, nor for that matter, her style.

Last night, I lost one of my sleeping pills in the bed, but I found it again this afternoon, fast asleep.

I haven't found any of the news believable since *1984*.

She couldn't string two words together without adding a third, and so on…

I often hear her muttering to herself, 'What an oaf…', and I think to myself, 'Oh, f…'

His genius said it all.

END OF DAYS

When I phoned my mother's new nursing home the nurse told me, "She's like a fish out of water."

I said, "Well, she is in her nineties and has led a full and active life surrounded by her family and younger friends, and so it's clearly going to be hard for her to adjust to a new quieter environment with people of her own age."

"No," she said, "she's dead."

There are three species on this planet able to survive freezing temperatures – penguins, polar bears, and a gaggle of young women on a hen party.

Whatever those young women in town were selling last night, the wrappers barely concealed the contents.

It's only a suspicion, but I think restaurant toilets are very dangerous places. I have lost count of the number of blind dates who have disappeared into them.

Rene Descartes was quietly getting drunk in a bar, and the landlord opined that he was becoming an alcoholic.

Rene replied, "I don't think I am", and disappeared.

---

iPhone therefore iTalk.

COMINGS AND GOINGS

Last month I received an invitation to a friend's 50th birthday party. The card called for *Fancy Dress*, which was a problem, not because of the furore such antics would have attracted, but because the dress I really fancied was far too revealing, and not only would I have to wax my designer chest stubble but also my bikini line. So, I stayed at home, at my exclusive *Singles* party.

———

After that last joke went viral at *The Flying Dutchman*, the police responded this month by moving me to their safe house, next door, and giving me a new identity and a gorgeous new wardrobe.

———

I have often wondered where ideas come from.

———

And why a preposition isn't a good word to end a sentence with.

———

In the condition I left the pub last night, it was staggering that I managed to get home.

———

I gave a street busker £10, on condition that he spent it on some music lessons.

———

The PM reshuffles his Cabinet again, but the pack is still full of jokers.

———

His ambitions were like clouds that would drift off into thin air before he could catch them, only to return unexpectedly, and catch him without his umbrella…

The secret of my success was abandoning all ambition.

THE IT INTERVIEW

Chairman: So, finally, why do you think you are the best applicant for our new Head of IT Security?

IT Nerd: Well, three reasons. One, I hacked into your systems, two, I replaced your shortlist with my name, and three, I am the only one here.

There are lies, damned lies, and government statistics.

HANDS UP

…anyone who wants to return this book for a refund?

…or anyone who has **never** seen a cyclist riding on the pavement, ignore traffic lights, use a phone while riding, ride the wrong way down a one-way street, or assault, curse, intimidate or scare a pedestrian?

So, no one, I see…

It's 99% of cyclists that give the rest of us a bad name.

LOOKOUT, IDIOTS ABOUT
2010
Dan Dare

sticker

The wife had gone out with her friends to a late-night screening of *Pride and Prejudice and Zombies* and left me at home alone, relaxing in my bath with a glass of fizz, when suddenly, I felt a tap on my shoulder...

My wife is always nagging me for leaving her to manage the household accounts. I thought of getting a divorce, but I knew I just couldn't face all that extra paperwork.

NEIGHBOURHOOD WATCH

Hello Sue

After you drove off this morning, I found your garage doors open, and I stepped inside. They juddered but remained open. I went inside further, in search of the control panel. Whilst there I tidied up the bedrooms and kitchen, rearranged your cutlery drawer, and fed all of those hungry dogs of yours before leaving again via the garage. This time they closed fully and appeared to be locked, suggesting to me that the dogs might have sabotaged them in order to be fed.

I think the lesson to be learned from this, is to make sure everything is shipshape before you abandon ship.

Tony

I should have realised my cheap electric car was too good to be true, after it stalled when the plug came out of the wall.

I don't suppose BJ's promised crackdown on crime will extend to serial adultery, lying to Queen and country, assaulting democracy, riding his bicycle on pavements, or displaying arrogance and ignorance.

––––––––

GRUMPY GRUMPS

Why is it that grandchildren always want to stay up well past your bedtime?

––––––––

I fitted a turbocharger to my time-reversal washing machine so that I could use it as a Time Machine, like Doctor Who's Tardis. On the outside, it's a compact white box, like any other kitchen appliance, but inside, it is head-spinning in its size. And not only is it fitted with all the mod-cons that I might need on my time-travels around the Universe, but it can also handle a month's load of washing, in next to no time at all.

––––

It can be tempting after a certain age, but one should always ensure that one has clean underwear every day. Paramedics are trained not to miss a thing.

––––––––

When a survey asked 1,000 Texan women what their favourite activity was, the first was sex and the morning commute was last, suggesting that none had ever travelled on London's Tube system in rush hour.

––––––––

2:30 – Dental appointment.

––––––––

LIFE'S DISAPPOINTMENTS

Psychiatrist: So, tell me Jack, why did you try to kill yourself?

Jack: Well, I was young, foolish, and totally in love with her. She was my perfect woman – gorgeous slim figure, long blonde hair, and great tits. We had two lovely kids, everything in the marriage was perfect, except she wanted driving lessons.

So, I booked her a course of ten, paid for them up front and before she was half-way through them, she drove off into the sunset with her instructor, and I never saw either of them again.

Psychiatrist: And how hurt were you by that?

Jack: Very hard. Especially as I'd just had the car serviced, and with a full tank it had a range of nearly 500 miles, and it was a drop-dead head-turner.

Psychiatrist: And what about the suicide itself, was it a serious attempt, a cry for help or simply an expression of your devastation?

Jack: I don't know, but it was pretty inept really. I had a large bottle of paracetamol tablets, a hundred, I think, and I took nearly all of them, which was far too many. But the problem was that the kids had managed to open the lid, and accidentally flushed them down the lavatory, and replaced them with Smarties so I wouldn't find out. And the clever little sods had licked all the colour off them but eaten all the brown ones, because if you have ever tried them, it's impossible to get all the colour off.

And in the dark, of course, by washing them down with the gin I had no idea. I was as sick as a parrot and so I called 999. They rushed me into hospital, gave me the stomach pump and here I am talking to you.

Psychiatrist: Well, you seem to have fully recovered now, and with your new car and new blonde, you're dealing pretty well with the emotional aspects of your loss. But tell me, and this is a standard question we ask all of our patients, do you ever think you might be related to the Queen?

Jack: No, but sometimes I think she might be related to me.

Psychiatrist: Well, she isn't, so clear off, you lunatic...

VIRGIN TERRITORY

Adam: That apple you gave me was rather bitter.

Eve: First of all, it was a metaphorical gesture that you completely failed to understand. Instead, you snatched it from me when it wasn't yet ripe or ready for eating, and my idea was that we share and enjoy a rather different pleasure together. Instead, you gobbled it all up so quickly, it stuck in your throat leaving you with that ugly lump, and leaving me with my first fruitless and disappointing experience.

Titillation: the artful practice of a woman slowly removing her bra.

I've discovered my girlfriend's bra is just a massive booby trap.

FIRST DATES

Eve: You had my apple, all to yourself, and all you've got to offer me is that tiny, miserable, shrivelled banana.

Adam: Well, it's just as well I don't have an inferiority complex yet, but that's only because I know you're not going to be offered anything better, anytime soon.

I met an attractive archaeologist at my college reunion, and after we got chatting, I asked her for a date.

She looked at me quizzically and said, "Well, it's difficult without my accelerator mass spectrometer, but I would say 1945 – 1947AD."

I abandoned my career in archaeology when it ended in ruins.

Beer Belly M: It's the wife that drives me to drink, you know.

Beer Belly L: In that case, do you think she'd mind picking me up on the way tomorrow evening?

If there is no God, I will be His Prophet.

A POINTLESS EXERCISE

Airport Security were very excited when they found and then confiscated a screwdriver that I had left in my work gilet pocket, thinking that they had foiled the first WASP terrorist, convincingly disguised as an old man.

But more to the point, and to drive home the blind stupidity of this paranoid fascism, or fascist paranoia, I only had to buy a box of sushi, on the airside concourse, to get two equally sharp, and potentially lethal, wooden chopsticks. And if I had been minded to do so, I could have sharpened them even further using the pencil sharpener from my innocuous artist's arsenal, that also included several mechanical pencils and a brand new set of crayons

———————

I was watching some kid's television last night, and this sleepy voice behind me said,
"Who are you, and what are you doing in my bedroom?"

———————

In the UK, debate has raged about a missing comma on the reverse of the new commemorative post-Brexit 50p coin, with everyone overlooking the missing 20% in its exchange value, making it worth only 40p.

————

Proof-reading my last book, I found an unnecessary comma, so I took it out and saved it for this one,

———————

Hell is other people, especially busloads of tourists.

———————

WAITING II
2018
Dan Dare

a solo performance

DISNEYWORLD

In the age of Trump, it's easy to forget that once upon a time, Americans were proud and confident enough to laugh at themselves with little embarrassment.

And so it was, way back in the days of Ronnie Reagan, when the family and I were on holiday in Florida doing Disneyworld's Magic Kingdom, EPCOT, and World Showcase. The last is a collection of national pavilions displaying the history and cultural achievements of various countries around the world, including America.

Now as anyone who has ever been to Disney knows, there is the tedious but efficient conveyor-belt queuing system for visitors to get into the various attractions. This involves shuffling along in snake formation, with minor entertainment and related warm-up highlights on route. Well, when we finally got out of the sun and into the shade of THE AMERICAN ADVENTURE pavilion, a colossus of a faux 19th century plantation estate house, we all thought we had finally arrived at the main attraction, whatever that was going to be.

The reality was that with about 500 other visitors, we had only been herded into the anteroom to the main auditorium in which a live musical performance was due to take place at the end of the current one. Well, we waited and waited with nothing to do, and nothing else to focus on except the closed doors before us. It was towards the end of this tedious wait that a middle-aged American voice observed to his companion,

"Jeez, I hope there's more to our country than this…"

Sumt fólk er svo fátækt allt sem þeir hafa eru peningar.

(Another Icelandic proverb)*

William Blake has portrayed *God as Architect*, but I wonder if he overlooked numerous other more obvious candidates. For instance, the efficiency and beautiful bone structure of the female body might point to Him being a structural engineer, or the efficiency of the human circulation and respiratory systems might suggest a mechanical services engineer. But I think the prime candidate has to be the council's city engineer.

After all, who else would place a lavatory slap bang in the middle of a playground.

Winston was the luckiest man alive, when he was knocked down on the pedestrian crossing outside the hospital by an empty ambulance.

His wife wasn't so lucky though. She smacked her head on the ceiling after she backfired.

Most things in life need time before you can appreciate them fully, with the exception, of course, of housework.

The world is a small place but not if you have to clean it.

(Some people are so poor all they have is money.)

I knew that Google tracks where we go every day, but I was caught with my trousers down when Maps' Timeline popped up on my phone this morning, to suggest I might be running low on toilet paper.

I had a handbag call from the wife last week.
I don't know who she had in there, but it sounded like they were having a jolly good time.

Then I had a video call from her last night and couldn't believe some of the things she carries in her handbag, like spare scanties – well, I hope they were spare ones.

Indian brave: Chief, how do you decide the names of new-born braves in our tribe?

Chief: Well, on the day of the birth, I recall the first thing I saw in the morning as I left my tee-pee, and that is the name I give him. Why do you ask, Little Dog Shitting?

He would go to church every day and spend an eternity arguing with God until He gave up.

His cremation was vital acclimatisation for his next destination.

It's sad that the cemeteries are full of people you never knew, or that they were ever alive.

My family and friends tell me I'm eccentric, just because I have one leg shorter than the other and move in odd circles, oh, and one hairy but well-groomed shoulder.

———————

NOSTALGIA 3

Many of you will be incredulous that in the 1950's, around the advent of television, the ventriloquist Peter Brough and his dummy Archie Andrews attracted huge radio audiences. And we all thought he was brilliant.

————

'How ridiculous,' I hear you say, 'a ventriloquist on radio. Anyone could do that'. And yet none of you will stop and question today's rash of TV cookery competitions with judges telling you 'how delicious it all smells and tastes'.

———————

As my last book was being finalised and signed off for printing, I realised my fussiness had stretched the publisher almost to breaking point. I apologised to her, and suggested that in celebration, she should now relax with her feet up, and maybe join me with a stiff one and my bottle of fizz ready to be popped.

————

The trouble with the *double entendre* is that it only has one meaning.

———————

After its successful 'Get Brexit Done' manifesto, the UK's one-man government now presents his policies as three-word slogans and whimsical rules.

———————

I usually find women with 'body art' a bit of a turn-off, but I've been seeing one recently who has Kama Sutra tattoos, literally all over her body. They are a real thriller with lots of twists and turns that I am just getting to grips with, and well, you can guess the rest...

When she objected that I was always trying to 'get into her knickers', I told her that if she went on a serious diet, her new ones would just be an impossible dream.

After centuries of suppression, anytime and anywhere she feels like, and for any reason at all, legally a woman can now just open her mouth and deliberately scream.

Only yesterday, I saw one screaming as she ran out of Prada carrying a pair of shoes and matching handbag. But on reflection, that was probably an uncontrolled one, like an orgasm.

Siegfried, the idiot product of incest, who would remain fearless until his first encounter with a woman, must have been enormously disappointed after fighting his way through a ring of fire to the top of the mountain, where, cutting off the helmet and breastplate of his newly discovered 'best friend', to find that 'he' was actually his Auntie Brünnhilde, whose hat and bra he had just whipped off while she was asleep, leaving him with another two mountains to scale

---

.Thank. goodness. my. full. stop. key. is. working. again.

She always had so much to say for herself, she rarely had time for punctuation.

JACK IN THE BOX...

Jack: Forgive me, Father, for I have sinned.

Priest: I hope this isn't another repeat of yesterday's confession and like last week's, another waste of my time, when you told me that you had given up drinking and smoking, and entertaining loose women, speeding and reckless driving without insurance, and handling stolen property, and taking time off work pretending to be at death's door, is it?

Jack: No, Father, that was all true, but I missed out the most important sin of all.

Priest: Okay, Jack, tell me what you forgot?

Jack: I also tell lies.

PUZZLING TIMES

When I travelled to work by train, I liked to impress my fellow commuters by completing the *FT* crossword in a record breaking five minutes every day. I would then fold the paper up and put it back in my briefcase.

What no one ever saw were my 'solutions'. Starting in the top left corner I would simply write out the alphabet, or my wife's shopping list, as best as I could recall it.

PUZZLE PAGE

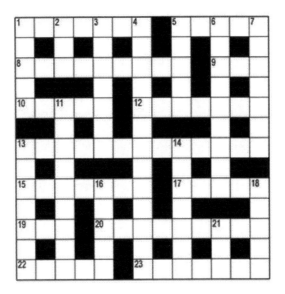

A CROSSWORD FOR THE CLUELESS

If you have found the book challenging so far, try completing this puzzle without the clues.

(Solution on page 148)

AN IDLE RESPONSE TO A CRITICAL REVIEW

Dear Sir or Madam,

I am sorry you were disappointed with the US preview paperback copy of my book, but allow me to address some of your complaints.

The format, size and page count are intended for a stylish European gentleman's jacket side pocket, without spoiling its lines, but with enough projection of the book above the pocket-line to allow one to grip and extract it without fumbling and the creasing of book or jacket.

The cover design, my own, is eye-catching in its very simplicity. If one looks at any bookstore or library shelf, one is visually bombarded into blindness by the cacophony of colour and graphics, all clamouring for one's attention. Whereas a white book with black text, and a simple graphic device linking the title to the author's name below, and which also illustrates the intangible, cerebral origins of its contents, will stand out in any crowded marketplace. And on further reflection is a touch of modest genius.

Cover robustness, or lack of, is a general weakness with paperbacks, which is why I have had a special edition print run of 200 in hardback for my closest friends. However, because of the excellent quality of the writing and of the UK printing, and an emerging melee of rediscovered close, but not so dear, friends jostling for VIP treatment, I have ordered an additional 50 deluxe paperback copies at a cost of £5 a throw plus p&p, for impromptu discounted sale to those lower down the batting order.

I can send you a copy, but there may be a bit of a wait for the second printing if there is one.

Regrettably, coloured illustrations would have doubled the printing costs, and priced it out of its market sector. And since the special edition are to be gifts to my friends, few of whom are as critical as yourself, I decided enough already.

Unless your copy has been badly bound, the margins should be 'industry standard', which supposedly are adjusted for the extra paper to be 'stitched' or 'double stitched', or in today's low cost, competitive market glued into the covers.

The paper weight and colour are also standard for black and white print books and not a problem for those who do not have to move their lips when reading. Heavier weight paper, often creme and aged looking, is used for readers with poor eyesight, or for those planning immediate personal recycling at home.

I do hope you have fun reading it, or having it read to you, and by the time you get to the end and start again, the only clue that it isn't a brand new and unread book will be its crumpled and tatty cover, no doubt complementing that of its reader.

Happy reading.

Jack

———

"Beware the man of a single book."

———

Dear Tony

I saw a pair of Queen Victoria's bloomers sold at auction in London for a record price. Was it you who snapped them up?

Jack

———

Hi, Jack

No, I didn't like the look of them. They were very worn and weren't 'fresh to the market', meaning they had been offered around privately a few times before.

They were also a little on the large side for me.

Tony

———

Bloke 1: My wife is an angel.
Bloke 2: Lucky you, mine's still alive…

———

Wife 1: Why is your wedding ring on the wrong finger?
Wife 2: I married the wrong man.

———

I always read my wife's horoscope first to see what kind of day I'm going to have.

———

When the missus stopped wearing her bra during the national house-arrest, I could see that it wasn't only her standards of dress that were slipping.

———

OUT OF AFRICA

In the early seventies in Southern Rhodesia, before it became Zimbabwe, I worked with a planning and architectural practice, and discovered the global similarities of humour.

The banter and repartee from our Shona colleagues rivalled anything we 'long-noses' would throw at them, with their great names like George, Cyprian, Sixpence, Wilfrid and Never, who no matter how many times we asked, would never tell us how he got his name, Never.

But most memorable was the time that our white chief surveyor Graham asked George, his deputy, why, like all other Af's, he had such a big bum. His answer was instant and direct – he 'needed a big hammer to drive in a big nail.'

Rearrange the following into their chronological order:

3. Judgement
4. Imprisonment
1. Parliament
2. Government

The sexy woman I met in a bar last night took me back to her place, and insisted we made love in the dark on her shag-pile carpet.

This morning I discovered the carpet was the contents of her husband's wardrobe.

Psychologist: What is your greatest weakness?
Paul Dirac: Interpreting the semantics of a question but ignoring the pragmatics.
Psychologist: Can you give me an example?
Paul Dirac: Yes.

"Reality exists in the human mind, and nowhere else."

On my wife's birthday, she was pessimistically reflecting on her age, until I suggested that she should just think of it as a legitimate opportunity to enjoy another cake.

The next day she announced that she was going to avoid everything that made her fat, like bathroom scales, mirrors, and selfies.

She: I wish you'd help me with the housework a bit more, instead of sitting there reading the newspaper.
He: You're beginning to sound like my ex-wife.
She: You never said you'd been married before.
He: I haven't.

My Gran was a regular church-goer and had a hot line to God, she once told me sitting on my knee. She said that He regularly sent horrible plagues to 'visit us' and that they came in alphabetical order, just like hurricanes, and when He got to the end of the alphabet, He started all over again. She warned me that when I reached her age, there was another one due, called Boris.

BLUNDERBUS

When Johnson was elected Mayor of London, like all egotists, he felt the urge to leave a memorable legacy, something that would be fondly remembered, like the old Routemaster bus that had allowed passengers to hop on and off at will, via the open rear platform.

So, he came up with his 'Boris Bus'. It was impractical, ugly, and unsafe, with doors at the front and middle, to speed up boarding and disembarking, and an open rear platform that would soon require a conductor, doubling its crew, to ensure that passengers only used it when safe to do so.

Equipped with hideous lighting, rear-facing seats, two staircases, poor ventilation and dangerous door traps that any competent designer would have avoided, the buses went into service, but soon underwent costly modifications to rectify their most serious shortcomings.

Finally, the fleet operators admitted defeat, abandoning another of the driving concepts of the design. In order to eliminate fare-dodging, passengers can now only board at the front door, with the other two as exits only, one of which is clearly redundant and nonsensical.

Less of a legacy, more of a backfire or farewell fart…

——

With his political downfall looming, I thought it only fair to the vacuous windbag, to draw people's attention to his unique intellectual capacity, and the achievements that have set him apart from the rest of us mere mortals…

——

BORIS JOHNSON'S GOOD IDEAS

EUREKA

At times, even your closest friends can surprise you with their ignorance or stupidity. Stephen opined that at 10%, architects' fees were ridiculously high in comparison with estate agents fees at 2%.

I sat him down, and explained that a surgeon is a highly trained professional specialist who has spent at least a decade learning how the human body works in all its intricate detail, how to diagnose correctly its many potential malfunctions, and then trained in the practical skills of keeping patients alive while repairing or replacing parts that were injurious to their survival. Whereas a sturgeon is a fish.

It reminded me of some Greek kid, I once met on my travels years ago, Archie, who thought that ships were filled with cork to keep them afloat, but he was barely ten years old at the time.

I can spend days in Stephen's library, where everything is meticulously catalogued under Miscellaneous.

For her birthday, my wife wanted a copy of Norwegian author Karl Ove Knausgaard's *THE END*, a paperback for casual reading on her numerous flights around Europe, but she has had to rethink her plan.
At 1,150 pages long, surely a record, it is heavy and thick enough to warrant its own suitcase, and long enough for a nonstop circumnavigation of the globe.

PUB TALK 2

He: So, Carmen, tell me how your parents came to be opera lovers, and why they named you after my favourite Bizet opera?

She: They weren't really; they christened me Mercedes, after my father's beloved car. And because I came to love cars, and I love men, and especially big men in big cars with big engines and big tailpipes, Carmen was an obvious nickname. What about you, what's your name?

He: Well, both my parents were classics scholars, so they christened me Titus Flavius Vespasianus, after the first century military commander who went on to become the Emperor of Rome. But being too much of a mouthful for most of them, my friends have taken to calling me...

She: No, let me guess, they call you Tits...

He: No, they call me Don.

She: Why Don? Isn't that a bit of a *non sequitur*?

He: Well, not really, it's shorter and less explicit than Donkey Dick.

Recently, my girlfriend has become a huge rugby fan, but when I asked her who had won the England-Ireland game, she didn't appear to understand the question.

Two Irishmen walked out of a pub.

A SURPRISE IN STORE

On a brief outing to my local Tesco, as I approached the checkout, the young 20+ year old cashier took a hurried swig of water from her bottle. As I put my half-price Mint Magnum ice creams on the belt, she spluttered and coughed uncontrollably, and in embarrassment then apologised for her inelegant lack of self-control.

Me: No problem, you're forgiven…

At this point, the 40+ year old customer who had just arrived behind me expressed her concern.

Lady: Are you sure you're okay?

Me: She's fine, I think she was just briefly overcome by my dashing good looks.

Cashier: No, it wasn't that. I had my mouth full and couldn't catch my breath.

Me: See, I told you, it happens to me all the time.

It's not only because of my own humble roots, but also the fine example set by my friend, Stoker, that I have learnt to treat all my staff as equals and with respect. From the gardeners up to my butler, Crouch, I like to ensure they have plenty of cake to eat, and not only at Christmas, and a jolly good novel to read in bed, but not, I hasten to add, anything by D H Lawrence.

Q: Does art matter?

Today, the art world has become vulgar and infected with money and politics, but fortunately great art is immune to both and always survives.

————

According to the famous TV art historian and nun, Sister Wendy, the Renaissance was all about the nude and its unadorned beauty, or as one contemporary art observer put it, less elegantly, dicks, tits, and smack-able bums.

————

Botticelli never married, and his Birth of Venus is widely regarded as his idealised woman, with beautiful long-flowing hair, modestly concealing but also revealing her slim figure and perfectly formed breasts, and those beautiful long, elegant hands, unmarred by housework.

————————

I've just been reading about an 'experiential pop-up' art show without any real art, but an entrance fee of £18.

Well, my original 'experiential pop-up' masterpiece offers any art-loving beauty an unforgettable experience, and it's free.

————

No art is complete until the viewer has responded to it.

————————

After Tom Hanks' convincing portrayal of the fictional film simpleton, Forrest Gump, he could turn his attention to a real one – Donald Trump.

————————

A: Only if there is intelligent life in the Universe.

GIVING HER AWAY 1

Good afternoon, Ladies and Gentlemen. We are running a little late so please carry on eating, but quietly.

It is a pleasure to see you all here today to celebrate Antonia and Paul's wedding, and my imminent discharge from her private institution where I have been held since she qualified as a Psychologist.

This is one of those occasions when a father is duty bound – to his daughter's eternal embarrassment – to entertain the gathering with humorous tales and anecdotes of her early life. So here goes…

Antonia was a child before her time – literally. She broke out of her pre-natal prison two weeks early, with a full head of hair which earned her the nickname Spike, and with a wail like a police siren.

Ten months later, she began walking, but not on *terra firma*. Her feet were actually 40,000 feet off the ground, *en route* to the Middle East, which was an early indication of Antonia's high ambitions and determination to go places.

At this time, Antonia's vocabulary really took off, too. Her first multi-syllabic words brought a tear to my eye – 'pocket money'. She knew what she wanted and how to get it, even then.

Upon her return to London three years later, she had her first lesson in people restraint at St George the Martyr Primary School, where she came under the tutelage of Miss Bennett, an old-fashioned Irish school ma'am, who used to moonlight as a martial arts trainer for Group 4 Security.

However, once she discovered that Antonia's family tree looked like an Irish phone directory - Durkin, Fitzgerald, McGeagh, McKevitt, Murphy, and even Wellington to boot, and an Irish road map - Boorston, Cork, Donegal, Longford, Sligo, Waterford, and Liverpoool, Miss Bennett relaxed her grip in a momentary weakness of kinship. This was Antonia's opportunity, and she absconded to All Souls, a somewhat more open school, but one still enclosed by a very high wall.

From there, Antonia won a place at the City of London School for Girls, targeted because she liked the uniform. Talking of which, I recall Antonia, who was very good at handicrafts, once making a police uniform for her Barbie doll.

For the unfamiliar, City School is a female institution deep in the bowels of London's Barbican Centre – Barbican being an archaic name for a fortified enclosure and further confirmation of Antonia's comfort zone.

It was here, at the age of thirteen, that she made her first intervention in the world of the criminally insane.

She and the other City schoolgirls had been the victims of the Barbican Flasher, something of which Jean and I had been completely oblivious, until one evening when the police knocked on the door to request Antonia's attendance at an identity parade of suspected flashers.

If anyone can actually picture such an event, hold that image and thought, while we take a natural break…

INTERMISSION

approx. 20mins.

for
toilet break
idle chit-chat
refreshments
phone-fiddling
eye-rolling

GIVING HER AWAY 2

And so, the identity parade took place, and became the model for some pretty awful TV programmes.

It was an open and shut case. Antonia identified the flasher by his singularly long red (cough) socks – caught 'red-footed', one might say, an achievement that earned her the epithet, Barbican Barbie.

That was probably Antonia's epiphany, a revelation that there were numerous men loose on the streets, who needed putting away.

Antonia is actually a very good artist and had been vacillating whether to pursue that as a career or to join the police, whose uniform (and truncheon) she liked.

When I declared my preference for her to be a penniless artist rather than to associate with 'the criminal elements of society', I think I used the word, 'scum', she chose psychology. So much for my guidance...

And so, step by step, or rather degree by degree, she embarked on a career in forensic psychology, with a brief interruption in Health Care Management.

At the ripe young age of 26, Antonia was appointed to the position of General Manager at Moorfields Eye Hospital, an old prison-like institution that ironically was missing its targets.

After three years of sorting out that problem, and collecting another degree in the process, she knew it was time to get back on track.

Taking a two-thirds cut in salary, a commendable sacrifice by any ambitious, highly paid young person, she began working as a psychology assistant, pursuing a series of placements at our major mental institutions where she could often be seen walking the corridors at night, playing tunes with her truncheon on the cell doors.

Antonia is actually a capable and versatile musician – firstly on the piano, then the trumpet, and now the truncheon.

It was at one of her placements, Broadmoor, that Antonia and Paul met. It was a lucky first encounter for both of them. They were acting as MasterChef judges of unstable inmates who were testing their culinary skills using real kitchen knives.

Now applying her truncheon technique to the piano and elsewhere around the home, she has formed a striking new partnership with guitarist Paul.

They plan a performance of their uniquely styled debut composition later this evening, when everyone is drunk, or departed if you are sensible.

There are many more stories with which I could regale you, but Antonia has redacted them and threatened to have me permanently 'sectioned' if I dare.

So, I will finish there, and before they start their musical performance, we should resume our anaesthesia.

Please be up-standing, raise your glasses, and toast the Bride and Groom…

———————

LETTER TO FT

15th March 2020

Dear Sir

In your editorial, *Britain's counter-virus strategy gamble*, you have revealed again our PM's truncated thinking.

Hopefully, if the advice to allow the virus to sweep through the country to establish a herd immunity is validated, the essential first step must be isolation of all the elderly and others at-risk. This could be achieved not by illegally putting them under house-arrest, but checking they are all virus-free with a short quarantine, and offering all of them the free cruise of a lifetime, out of harm's way, leaving the remaining 'more able-bodied' to establish the immunity for all, for however long that may be effective. It is clearly better to spend your resources on prevention than cure, which is cheaper and healthier, and avoids further burdens on our NHS.

A private cabin to the US eastern seaboard from where I could wave my Union Jack would offer a welcome respite from the current paranoia.

Jack Idle

———

My new senior's bus pass arrived today with an expiry date five years hence, same day as my hip operation.

———

"We are going to make a Titanic success of Brexit."

———

TEST PILOT OF THE FUTURE

An early teething problem with my prototype time-reversal
washing machine was the calibration of the programme
timer. The first time I used it, I wrongly guesstimated when
I had bought the shirts. As a result I overestimated the
time needed to restore them to their original condition.
And when I opened the door, the drum was filled with fluffy
white cotton balls, and with no sign of the shirts I assumed
the balls had yet to meet their maker.

And then I wondered, what would happen if I went for a
spin in it, and in which direction, backwards or forwards.

––––

And my second problem was women. Many had already
spotted the potential of a larger machine, and pestered
me to build one and include an 'anti-wrinkle' function.

––––––––

THE CIRCUS COMES TO WESTMINSTER

Even as a child, when I loved the circus for its clowns
and their outrageous appearance and idiotic antics,
I knew that none of them would ever be suitable as the
Ringmaster, with the management overview and ability
to hold the show together and keep it on the road.

––––––––

"This wallpaper is killing me; one of us has to go."

––––––––

Since Brexit, I've had to drink champagne by the gallon.

––––––––

AMAZON REVIEW 2

The Ski-Bag.

An excellent, spacious bag for the price, and the absence of padding allows it to be rolled up when not in use.
It has many other uses too – carrying rolled up works of art around the world without drawing the attention of nosey money-grabbing customs officers, and for smuggling diminutive underfed Romanian tumblers into Britain. This amazing duo have now joined Billy Smart's Circus, drawing big crowds, and making a lot of money without relying on our DHSS. They periodically drop by to thank me, and ask to climb into the bag again, 'for old time's sake'. It was a tight fit though, due to a slight weight gain, but it was surreal watching the bag ripple like a snake as they wriggled around inside it trying to get comfy. Cute!

Jack Idle

––––––––––

My girlfriend has been a Formula 1 fanatic ever since Michael Schumacher winked at her and blew her a kiss. So finally last year and at great expense, she signed up for one of those supercar driving experiences, and because she was a woman, she had first pick of all the cars every man lusts after – Bugatti, Ferrari, McLaren, Mercedes-AMG, Porsche – and a pink car…

––––––––––

I am not sure which came first, Stephen's stammer or his knighthood.

––––––––––

DRESS CODE

Dr A: Good morning, Mr Idle, how are you today?

Jack: I really struggled to get out of bed this morning to get the bus to the surgery to see you. I suppose I am OK, but feel rather depressed, lacklustre, and lethargic. And my friends rarely come around to visit me anymore or invite me out to dinner. Is there something you can prescribe, a tonic perhaps to lift me out of the doldrums and get me going again?

Dr A: Well, I can see you do have a problem. It's not a tonic you need, but a more positive approach to living life to the full, and it would help if you started with a clean dressing gown and a pair of matching slippers.

———————

The problem with Quantum Theory is that after you have read a few books on the subject, as many people do, and then think you understand it, you know you haven't.

————

His mind worked on a different plane, like the old Concorde now grounded at Heathrow with a flat tyre.

———————

Doreen of Lee near Blackheath was an evil old crone. She earned a living childminding and cat-sitting and maliciously lied to people and even the police about anyone who crossed her or her path, while at the same time claiming state-benefits until long after she died.

I guess even in Hell, she wanted free money to burn.

————

Your reference:

Our reference:

Date: 26 May, 2015

Metropolitan Police Service
Child Abuse Investigation Team

Mr █ H█████
██████████
London
████████

Marlowe House
Station Road
Sidcup
Kent
DA15 7ES.
Metline: 020 7230 3121

Dear Mr H██████,

As per our telephone conversation of today, I write to confirm that no action will be taken against you in respect of a 3rd party allegation of inappropriate touching in respect of Ms G████ ██████ ██████.

The allegation was unfounded and as such you have been eliminated from the enquiry. A computer record of the investigation has been detailed under reference 3209172/15.

I trust that this letter will put your mind at rest after the distress the allegation has caused you and G██████. I also hope that you will be able to tickle each other as much as you like, and for as long as G██████ can stand it. However, you should both be careful that those sad busybodies living in Blackheath do not get to hear about your activities. They are a funny bunch for whom tickling is no laughing matter, and they are best avoided. And, if D███ should ever venture over there again, for her own good she should take her used tea-leaves home with her.

If you encounter any resistance from G██████, let me know and I'll send you a set of bracelets for her.

Kind regards and happy tickling.

Detective Sergeant
L██████ G████████

Working for a safer London

CERTIFICATE OF INNOCENT INNOCENCE
2015
Dan Dare

Redacted MR photocopy

79

THE WORLD IS A STAGE INDEED

General Manager
Old Vic Theatre
London SE1

Dear Sir/Madam

You may be interested in, perhaps inspired by, the following transcript of events on the evening of 22nd December 2016.

Setting: Old Vic Foyer, Thursday evening before Christmas.

Act 1, Scene1.

Mr Homes, a retired gentleman with a legal background and accidental patron of the arts, enters stage right with his diminutive but fearsome housekeeper, Mrs Hudson. He immediately strides towards the young programme seller, Miss Carey, stage left. Picking up a programme from the top of a pile on the counter, he asks the young lady, "Is this the programme and how much is it?"

Miss C, turning away towards a colleague, or perhaps the wall, mumbles, "Yes, £4."

Mr H. places the programme in his bag and fumbles to extract four £1 coins from his shiny new coin holder and offers it to Miss C, now facing him again.

Miss C: "Have you got one?"

Mr H: "Yes thank you. And you said they were £4."

Miss C: "They are. Have you got a programme; did you take one?"

Mr H: "Yes, I did, thank you."

Miss C: "Where is it?"

Mr H: "In my bag."

Miss C: "I want to see it."

Surprised by her terse demand, Mr H. asserts: "I have one; it's now in my bag; here's the m..."

Miss C. robustly interrupts, "I need to see in your bag before I take your money."

Mr H. replies, emphatically, "You aren't looking in my bag. I have told you I have one, and here is the money."

Miss C. rejects the coins and excitedly repeats her demand, "I need to see it, in your bag, before I can take the money."

Mr H. turns to walk away, saying, "You are not looking in my bag. Take the money, or don't. It's up to you."

Miss C. now very agitated, shouts at him, "Give me the money, then."

Mr H. turns, politely hands over the four £1 coins to Miss C, turns around shaking his head, and with Mrs H, exits stage right.

– *Intermission* –

Act 2, Scene 1.

Twenty minutes or so later, Mr H. and Mrs H. are standing quietly centre stage waiting for their friends to appear. The Duty Manager, Mr Dim enters stage left and approaches Mr H.

(The following exchange is a summary to avoid an early onset of narcolepsy.)

Mr D speaks (*sotto voce*): "I want to speak to you about your shouting and swearing at my staff."

Mr H: "Pardon?"

Mr D: "You shouted and swore at a member of my staff and upset her."

Mr H: "No, I didn't."

Mr D: "She says you did, and so does her colleague."

At this point Mrs H who had been a silent extra during Scene 1 interjects, "No, he did not. He raised his voice in response to her talking over him, and he never swore at her. He's a gentleman and never swears at anyone."

After briefly exiting stage left, Mr Dim returns and says, "She is sticking to her story." And (*sotto voce* again), "You called her a 'stupid bitch'."

Mr H thinks to himself, 'An apt description – pointlessly chasing her own tale.'

Mrs H: "No, he didn't."

Mr D: "She says he did. She was in tears, and I have to believe her."

Mrs H: "No, he didn't, and no you don't."

Mr D: "Oh yes, he did."

Mrs H: "Oh no, he didn't"

Mr D: "Did."

Mrs H: "Didn't."

etc, etc...

Bored, Mr H strolls off and exits stage right to find his friends helplessly rolling in merriment in the wings.

Act 3, Scenes 1 – 17.

A disappointing restaging of Yasmina Reza's play, *ART*, lacking the gentlemanly and cultured style of the London premier production some years ago, and marred by the gratuitous littering with contemporary street language, and the vandalising of the subject artwork, both of which were implausible given the sophistication of their characters that are key to the plot.

Regrettably, the first half of the evening remains the more memorable. Had the staging of the latter called for a challenging female part, it may have been adeptly met by your programme seller's latent thespian talents. It would certainly have kept her out of direct contact with me, and any other unfortunate member of the public.

My other observation on the evening is that contrary to his belief your Duty Manager's first responsibility must surely be for the safety, well-being and comfort of your patrons, and not for his staff as he stated. They would come second. Furthermore, as a Manager he needs to understand that any sustainable decision or verdict by anyone is only valid after all the available evidence has been gathered and rationally weighed. Anything else is irrational or prejudice.

All in all, an extraordinary and sorry tale. Should I ever feel the need to return to the Old Vic, methinks it will be safer to leave my satchel at home and instead don something less interesting – my extravagantly oversized codpiece, perhaps.

Yours faithfully

Jack Idle

————

Behind every boring old raconteur there is usually a woman rolling her eyes.

————

He frequently dreamt of reality, but it always eluded him, even when he woke up.

————

A Scouser went to see his doctor about his kleptomania and asked her if there was anything he could nick for it.

————

To quote the oft quoted Paul Dirac, "No."

————

GO STRAIGHT TO GAOL

Inspired by BJ's brilliant wheeze for circumventing the law, I have just paid my income tax bill with an unsigned cheque and a cover note telling them I really don't want to pay it.

God created Satan to give Himself a scapegoat, plus a few spares here and there.

BBC BROKEN NEWS: THE BODYSNATCHERS

After the UK government's failure to boost organ supplies with its Automatic Organ Donor (AOD) legislation, commonly known as the Burke and Hare Act, it has introduced a Bill to bring back Capital Punishment for murder and a variety of lesser crimes, including, but not limited to, shoplifting and illegal parking.

Meanwhile, there is a second reading of a Bill to make euthanasia legal, and even compulsory for those reaching retirement age, still able to walk unaided and demonstrate 20/20 vision etc, etc, and which will have the bonus of eliminating the state pension shortfall.

Despite my prior willingness to have my body recycled, I immediately opted out of this blatantly fascist state-ownership claim over my body, and despite my disapproval of such things, I popped down to the local tattoo parlour today and joined the long queue for their latest offering.

JACK'S TATTOO
2019
Dan Dare

tattoo

SOYLENT GREEN

Tony went down to his local hospital to sign his AOD opt-out papers, and that was the last we saw of him.

———

It is only a matter of time before we have compulsory euthanasia, but not in my lifetime, I hope.

———

And to those unthinking idiots who assume they know better, and are 'only thinking of other people's welfare', you have opened the gate on human farming.

———

SCARRED FOR LIFE

Before I could even walk, I burnt my forehead badly on the oven door, but in later years being sanguine about it, I saw it as only adding to my rugged good looks, and never gave it a second thought. Until one day in the office after a gloriously sunny weekend, my glamourous young assistant spotted its rather strange yellow colour.

"Oh my God, did you have an accident?" she exclaimed.

"No," I said, "it was 'domestic violence' a long time ago."

Of course, she immediately assumed it was of the worst kind, and something to do with my wife's long-handled 30 cm. diameter, non-stick handbag…

———

To quote the oft quoted Paul Dirac, "Don't know."

———

Mother: Well, that's the summer holidays over, and now it's back to school again, so no rushing but don't be late.
Children: But, Mummy, it doesn't open until next week…

———

When I told the wife that I was going back to college to study astronomy, she laughed at me and told me, as a Pisces, she didn't believe in any of that old nonsense.

———

He offered her total devotion, which she squandered on herself, before she tossed him aside like one of the used condoms.

———

After she got what she came for she didn't hang around.

———

The last time I dressed in a hurry, the paramedics called me 'Madam'.

———

HIGHWAY CODE?

Whether I am hurtling down the motorway or just tootling along in the outside lane holding everyone up, if I see anyone in the inside lane, which is very rare indeed, I think to myself, 'What a cissy…'

———

"Everybody wants to go to heaven, but few want to die."

———

Perhaps the lunatic is simply a minority of one.

———

Over the years I had come to believe that British Airways was run by Basil Fawlty, but on my last flight one of the cabin crew revealed that he had been replaced by his clueless assistant, Manuel.

My three-year-old grand-daughter's nursery enquired about her interests at home, so that they could include some of them in class to stimulate her interest and mental development.

Her mother responded with, "Peppa Pig, the genesis of Impressionism in the late 19th century, and the mechanical principles and spin-off potential of the domestic washing machine."

WOMEN AND CHILDREN FIRST

To guarantee her rescue in the event her Norwegian fjord cruise ship hit an iceberg and sank, an old friend of mine insisted on going to bed every night wearing a lifejacket and full make up.

I am not sure which of my wife's formidable range of weapons I fear the most – the withering look, the icy silence, her frying pans, or her new iris-scanning bedroom entry-phone.

When Ron called me to say he was stuck on a train, I didn't realise it was his way of telling me he had joined Extinction Rebellion…

When Ronnie Reagan appeared on the political scene, I recall thinking, 'This cannot be really happening, a Hollywood movie star as President of the USA?', but in real life he revealed himself to be an informed gentleman with humour, modesty, vision, and wit.

The current one is a cartoon character straight out of *Wayne's World* or *Beavis and Butthead*.

———————

I have often been described as 'puerile', which suits me if it keeps me alive and prolongs the fun.

———————

Imagine being a teetotaller, getting up and knowing that's as good as you are going to feel all day.

———————

I only fly because it's as close to God as I'm likely to get.

———————

I promised the wife I'd conjure up something fabulous for dinner tonight, so I bought two loaves and a fish.

———————

Why is fiction the opposite of fact, and not fict? And why isn't faction the opposite of fiction?

———————

I found a piece of petrified wood today, hiding in my rock collection.

———

"There is nothing to fear but fear itself," I'm afraid.

———————

Recently I visited Edinburgh for the first time. It's a nice city with grand buildings and charming people, and what's more, I only heard the bagpipes being practiced once, and to my surprise, by a large burly, bearded lady.

I was on the beach chatting to a beauty who had the skimpiest bikini I had ever seen. We were clearly getting on very well, until her two-metre, 100kg, tattooed boyfriend turned up and told me to clear off, which I did, thinking to myself 'that was a close shave.'

It may be a statement of the obvious, but brave men don't run in my family.

FIX THE FUNDAMENTALS FIRST

Mozilla recently asked us, *inter alia,* if we cared that our democracy may be about to be broken for good. But completely missing the point that society tends to get what it deserves, whether it is architecture, environment, culture or government, all of which reflect society's standards at the time.

It needn't be so. But the internet has made society shallower, more self-centred, more gullible, and more impressed and obsessed with trivial nonsense than ever before. And one of the proofs that supports this observation is the predictable bombast and rhetoric that passes for debate by the leaders of the three main UK political parties, and the racing certainty that people will still vote for them in their droves.

LOST IN SPACE AND TIME

String theory is a theoretical framework in physics in which the point-like particles of particle physics are replaced by one-dimensional objects called 'strings.'

Depending on which branch of the theory is under examination, it describes how these strings propagate through space and interact with each other, in ten, eleven or even twenty-six spacetime dimensions, instead of the familiar four of the physical world.

By page two of the simple beginner's guide, my brain was completely tied up in knots.

Democracy is a utopian dream of avoiding a dystopian nightmare.

DAVID OG GOLIATH

In the 1970's, Iceland and the UK stubbornly engaged in further disputes over fishing rights within Iceland's claimed territorial waters.

There were many confrontations in which both navies fired shots and rammed each other's vessels, incurring two accidental deaths and extensive damage. Things finally calmed down when the Royal Navy retreated after almost sinking under the weight of the potatoes that the Icelanders had thrown at them, shouting,

"The cod's finished, but have some more chips."

A DECEMBER DRIVE AROUND ICELAND
2017
Dan Dare

performance video still

DOUBLE STANDARDS OR POLICE STATE?

A 64-year-old man who lost his temper at a Swiss police station and told a policeman he was an 'arsehole' has been fined CHF1,100 (~£850). Why the man was upset is not clear. What is clear, however, is that the policeman took exception to the comparison and filed a complaint.

The local public prosecutor agreed with the policeman and concluded that the insult had been uttered 'knowingly and deliberately' and had 'violated the policeman's honour', by falsely or mistakenly claiming that the officer was the same size as his anus.

However...

Calling someone a 'foreign pig' and 'filthy asylum seeker' are insults, but do not violate Swiss anti-racist legislation, the country's Federal Court has ruled.

The court had been considering an appeal by a policeman against a suspended fine imposed by a court in Basel for insulting an Algerian whom he had detained on suspicion of bag-snatching. When the policeman was going through his papers and discovered that he was an asylum seeker, he used the words in the presence of numerous bystanders.

The court found that the terms did not violate the anti-racist law because they were not directed at a specific ethnic group or religion. It also said that using the word 'pig' or 'filthy' followed by a reference to a person's nationality was not a violation of the law either.

AMAZON REVIEW 3

Henry the Explorer: a children's adventure book.

A real ripping yarn that I couldn't put down, even when I fell asleep, but not enough rabbits or spaceships…

Jack Idle

After I saw the mounting piles of dirty dishes and ironing, and realised I hadn't seen the wife for about a week, I finally reported it to the police who told me that I should be prepared for the worst. So, I returned to the charity shops and bought back all her clothes.

If the government is serious about tackling climate change and waste, perhaps it should start with a ban on all junk mail – paper and digital.

Ron's girlfriend breathed a sigh of relief when her IQ test came back negative.

Psychiatrist: Tell me, Winston, do you think that your wife dominates you, and controls your life?

Mrs Smith: No, he doesn't.

"To be born a gentleman is a privilege, to die one is an honour."

SONG THRUSH

I have just seen a TV advert with a woman singing the praises of 'Canestan Thrush Duo', and now that it has cured her problem, she says she is 'unstoppable'.

She sounded like my kind of woman – ready for action.

BUSINESSWOMEN

She said they had singly attended the same business conference, and separately checked into adjoining hotel rooms that turned out to be the premier suite, and their discussions only broke down after he hogged the duvet.

Now that she was competing on her own terms in a man's world and had her own business to run, she knew that time was money, and she couldn't afford to waste either on fools, non-performers, or underwear.

The gaggle of excitable young women on my train today were so noisy, I thought I was at an orgasm recital.

To defend his country, the General ordered his troops to remain in barracks and avoid being overrun by the enemy, and remain able to defend the country.

No Semites, neither Arab nor Jew, were injured, killed, or even mortally offended during the writing of this book.

NOSTALGIA 4

I was lying in bed idly thinking about the shameless
dishonesty in politics today, and about the political
figures during my lifetime who had impressed me with
their honesty and other admirable qualities, like
Churchill, Thatcher, William Hague, probably the best
PM we never had, Tony Benn and Rory Stewart, and
finally Benito Mussolini.

But his name only popped up because for a long time
I thought he was an Italian seafood pasta.

The problem with predictive text is that it tends to reveal
how idiotic we have become.

MY END IS NIGH

With her phone constantly engaged with calls and texts,
I sent my wife an email to suggest dates for some
overdue conjugal activity, but I never got a response.

It turned out it had been diverted into Spam, and I was
no longer on her Allowed list with automatic access to
her Inbox.

When I was much younger, I was an early riser in the
mornings, but nowadays she's already downstairs, with
her attention and enthusiasm now turned to her oven
baked croissants, which she has accidentally described
as 'fresh and virile'.

She was a generous and big-hearted lady, with a wardrobe to match.

Beer Belly XL: I don't know about you, but right now I could murder a pint.

Beer Belly XXL: You can say that again...

Beer Belly XL: Okay, I don't know about you, but right now I could murder a pint – again.

Beer Belly XXL: Great, a double round then.

STRANGERS?

Sometimes I think the world is full of strange people, like the guy who phoned me last week about my 'three-piece suite' and asked if I would meet him in the park at midnight to show it to him. He still hasn't bothered to show up, even a week later.

And to counter any suspicion about which way I lean, a lady, this time, was also interested in my three-piece after her husband had kicked her out of the house, leaving her with nothing to sit on. After trying it out once, she was so impressed, the next day she turned up on my doorstep with a large and overflowing wardrobe.

My friends Ali and Mo are still in jail after they tried to sign up for a crash course in flying.

ROAMING CHARGES

Russian researchers were tracking migrating eagles using attached SMS transmitters, but ran up huge phone bills after the birds flew into Iran and Pakistan.

PREMIER TABLE

For Christmas, the grandsons wanted a new table football, not your pub league variety, but a hi-tech version with top-flight cup-winning teams, international stars, and no injury-prone diving wimps, but removable players in case of injury or the ref. red-carding someone, and to avoid on-pitch disputes, VAR of course...

AN EXPENSIVE HOMOPHONE

It was probably my own fault for never listening to her properly, but after I said 'bye-bye' to the wife as she left yesterday, I was horrified to find on her return today, she had been out and 'bought, bought, bought'.

In the civilised world, culture, truth, and evidence-based science will eventually trump all the bombast, lies and ignorance of politicians and their idiot supporters.

I apologise if my facts interfere with your ignorance.

Science is impervious to any nonsense you believe in.

THE STANDARD MODEL OF PHYSICS

$$\mathcal{L} = -\frac{1}{4} F_{\mu\nu} F^{\mu\nu}$$

$$+ i \bar{\psi} \slashed{D} \psi + h.c$$

$$+ \psi_i y_{ij} \psi_j \phi + h.c$$

$$+ |D_\mu \phi|^2 - V(\phi)$$

DISCUSS.
2020
Dan Dare

blackboard

103

Instead of constantly telling me off for every minor misdemeanour, I told my wife I'd prefer it if she just chalked them up on her blackboard each day, and at bedtime, gave me one jolly good spanking.

———

The other night after a rare bout of conjugal activity, I jumped out of my skin when she suddenly woke up.

———

An expert is someone who knows more and more about less and less.

———

America is a mongrel nation of natives, slaves, refugees and immigrants, resisting invasion by a world of aliens.

———

Even the legendary reliability and punctuality of the Swiss railways is now a thing of the past.

———

I'm disappointed the future isn't what it used to be.

———

The future can be changed by changing the present, but the past is history and its deeds can never be undone.

———

Google: the search engine that simultaneously searches your data and then sells it.

———

'Lord, what fools these mortals be!'

———

STANDARD MODEL OF PHYSICS (in 100 words)

The standard model of physics is a set of equations
that purports to explain the physical world, insofar as
our present observations and understanding allow.
In its detail it goes on to feature a table of sub-atomic
particles, invisible to the naked eye, that include, *inter
alia*, bosons, electrons, fermions, leptons, gluons, muons
and in the case of photons, visible particles, or waves.
But the model is recognised as patently incomplete,
since it fails to incorporate gravity, and offers no ideas
on the nature of dark matter and dark energy which
together account for around 95% of the total universe.

However, there is some speculation that this 'missing'
matter might simply be made up of far more of the
previously unknown particles than might have otherwise
been expected – morons.

––––

The laws of physics mean that our very existence on the
planet is inescapably contributing to global warming, as
demonstrated by the usual political rhetoric.

––––––––

Those who cast their votes count for nothing, whereas
those who count their votes count for everything.

––––––––

Interviewer: So, tell me, Jack, in fifty words or so, how
would you describe yourself?

Jack: Idle.

––––––––

LETTER TO TRANSPORT FOR LONDON

Dear Sir/Madam

Despite the thoughtful provision of signs on your Underground trains indicating priority seating for 'those less able to stand or in greater need', I have observed on numerous occasions that such seats are frequently occupied by children, younger citizens and others who are clearly able-bodied, who either genuinely bury their noses in their six-inch screens, or feign unawareness of the needs of their fellow passengers.

In short, your strategy is largely ineffective.

May I suggest you introduce a much simpler and effective alternative code of conduct that might also encourage more civilised behaviour generally, namely, denying use of any seat to anyone holding a mobile device in their hands or wearing earphones, whatever their age or dubious incapacity.

Yours faithfully

Jack Idle

———————

When I call my girlfriends, I put them on speakerphone, so that while we are chatting and without objection or offending them, I can stare at their chests.

———————

Our lives are trees of possibilities bound only by space, time, and propriety.

———————

RADIO HELP LINE

"Hello, you've reached Radio Station NPB Help Line. My name is Bob. How can I help you today?"

"Hello, Bob, my name is Roxy, and I need your advice. This morning I left home for work as usual, leaving my husband Ted in bed watching *Breakfast TV*. Two miles down the road my car stalled and refused to start again. With the car battery and my phone both dead, I walked back home to get my husband's help. When I got there, I was horrified to find Ted still in bed, and with my neighbour's teenage slut of a daughter. After she got dressed and left, he admitted that they had been having an affair for over a year and that they were 'in love' and wanted to get married. He refuses to discuss the matter of his casual betrayal, and that there is a twenty-year age difference. I am distraught, and I feel abandoned, and unable to recover. What should I do?"

"Well Roxy, it's a sad and common situation in which many women can find themselves, due to their reliance on things they don't fully understand, which inevitably let them down from time to time when they least expect it. So, for starters, I would recommend that you carry a spare battery for your phone and try to keep it fully charged for such emergencies. You should also ensure that your car is regularly maintained by an authorised agent, or by a knowledgeable and trusted friend. And failing the latter, if you let me have the make, model and registration number, if you can recall them, and where you abandoned it, it would be my pleasure to return the car to you, and make sure all of your batteries are fully charged, and you're ready for action."

The Daily Star was so impressed with my girlfriend they had no choice but to give her a full two-page spread.

———

Gravity is a serious matter for the well-endowed woman.

———

In 2019, aircraft fatalities fell by 50% over the previous year, living proof of the effectiveness of airport security.

———

Women often complain that the world is ruled by men, but mostly by men who are themselves ruled by women.

———

My friend Mel told me the last time she had a sexual encounter, it was like the men's Olympic 100m final, all over in ten seconds, and well, you can guess the rest.

———

It is currently in vogue for people, whatever their age or lack of expertise, to inculcate us with a concern for 'climate change' and the need to leave our planet habitable for our children.

Fair enough, but perhaps we should be equally, if not more concerned, about the kind of children we want to leave behind to look after it.

———

"Never use a long word when a short one will do."

———

I try to avoid clichés like the plague.

———

THE AGE OF ENLIGHTENMENT

Old Dear 1: I wish I was back in my old two-up two-down where I never saw any rats in my life.

Old Dear 2: Are you telling me you've got rats up on the 16th floor?

OD1: I have, lots of them, and I don't know how or where they've come from.

OD2: They must have used the lifts to get that high.

OD1: Yes, but how do they reach the buttons or know which ones to press?

OD2: They've been spying on us for years, just waiting for us to turn our backs...

OD1: Don't be ridiculous, and what about reaching the buttons...

OD2: They could have stood on each other's shoulders, you know, like a troop of acrobat-rats that have run away from the circus...etc, etc.

———————

Recently, I've noticed we now have as many potholes in our local roads as speed bumps, and not only are they related to each other, they appear to be breeding.

———————

The road to Hell is paved with traffic management disasters.

————

THIS IS NOT THE WAY

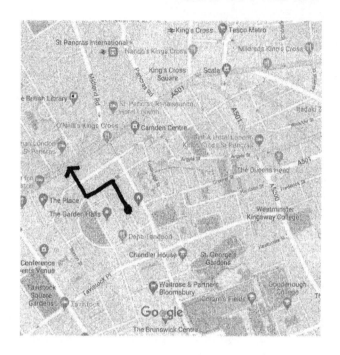

BEFORE TRAFFIC MANAGEMENT
Route = 0.2 mile
old route to start of journey
2020

Dan Dare

WE SHOULD ADDRESS CLIMATE CHANGE

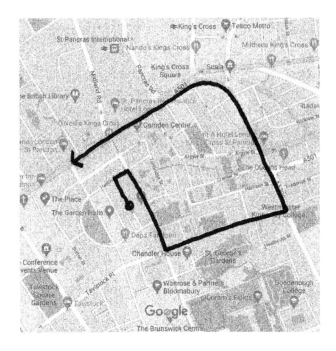

AFTER TRAFFIC MANAGEMENT
Route = 1.2 miles
new route to start of journey
2020

Dan Dare

1 1 1

THE ROADS TO RUIN

I have been banging on about idiot traffic planners and their highway engineers for years to no avail, but just think about this recent lunacy.

Not daring to put up any counter arguments to their idiot political paymasters, in response to terrorism one bunch duly butcher London's bridges with massive concrete and steel anti-truck barriers, blindly ignoring low-key alternatives. Meanwhile, another bunch is merrily reducing kerb heights in Mayfair, making it easier for the same trucks to drive on the pavements, obliviously facilitating and inviting terrorists to switch their targets.

THE XMAS QUIZ

He: Here's a simple one for you. What is the favourite colour of most women?

She: That's a typically sexist and insulting question to ask any woman. Why don't you ask me something a little more intellectually demanding, and which I might surprise you by knowing the answer to?

He: Okay then. Since the Big Bang almost 13.8 billion years old, ignoring any immeasurable and unknown cumulative effects that the period of inflation and dark energy may have contributed to the speed of light, c., and assuming that c. has been constant since then, what is the theoretical approximate diameter of the observable Universe?

She: Pink…

…and in answer to your second question, 93 billion light years, or 5.5×10^{23} miles. But some of this is beyond our current observational capabilities, and will remain so, as will the full extent of the actual Universe, which is both incalculable and probably unknowable, at least for now.

———

If you don't know what's happening out there in the Universe, you must have been reading the newspapers.

———

Research is what you are doing when you don't know what you are doing.

———

My children laugh at me because they think I'm insane. I laugh back at them, because in my case I know it's hereditary.

———

In his writing, the author David Mitchell draws inspiration from his 'compost heap' of ideas, while I lie buried up to my neck in society's landfill-site of stupidity.

———

FUTURE LIBRARY

Bonfire of the Scanties
A Nicer History
Dictionary of Banned Words
The Unholy Bible
Post-Annihilism
Is this a book, Grandma?
Reading for Beginners

———

LETTER TO FT

Sir

Informative and thorough as Simon Kuper's excellent *Politics and Sport* article was (21/22.12.2019), perhaps he should have included gender, race, and religion to complete his comparative analysis. That would have explained the underlying and ever-present tribalism.

Jack Idle

A CLOSE ENCOUNTER OF THE THIRD KIND?

After a long and intoxicating Christmas day at my daughter's home and with my granddaughter tucked up in bed, it was finally time to head home myself. As I stepped out into the cold night air, I looked up at the clear moonlit sky, and wondered if we were truly alone in this Universe, and if not, why have we not yet encountered more advanced alien visitors. Just then, I spotted a strange cluster of beautiful blue flashing lights hovering overhead, before they accelerated upwards in formation and sped off over the horizon. No, I thought, after too much Christmas cheer, you imagined them.

Usually a ninety-minute journey, I arrived home in a record-breaking fifty-five minutes, mainly due to the light motorway traffic that appeared to be going the wrong way as I weaved my way through it, the return of those flashing blue lights in my rear view mirror, and several impromptu cross-country shortcuts, as I left them with their wailing sirens in ditch after ditch…

AMAZON REVIEW 4

The Timewaster Diaries by Robin Cooper.

Dangerously hilarious.
The book arrived today on time, probably in good
condition. However, the packaging had been booby-
trapped by the inclusion of an unseen and unnecessary
partially inserted staple, upon which I inadvertently
stabbed myself, resulting in copious bleeding over the
package and its contents.
After my discharge from A+E, I returned home reflecting
on how narrowly I had escaped death.
I have now added a codicil to my will that my precious,
blood-stained book be placed in my mausoleum when
my time comes.

Jack Idle

Last year a London newspaper asked the question:

Are all voters as important as each other?

You only have to glance at the intellectual calibre,
competence, honesty and morality of those we have
managed to install in high office, almost everywhere in
recent years, to see that the answer to this rhetorical
question is that whatever their political persuasion, the
most important voters are the gullible.

She: Sorry, did you say something just then?
He: No, it was just another backfire.

I went into my local bookshop and had to ask where
I could find the fiction classics that I was interested in
– *Brave New World, The Handmaid's Tale, 1984,* and
Kafka's *The Trial.*

They told me they were now upstairs under Non-Fiction.

––––––––––

My good ideas always seem to come to me at bedtime,
with the best inspired by my glamorous companions.

––––

In Jack's excitement at finding his perfect woman, he fell
at the first hurdle, without even getting a leg over.

––––––––––

PSALM 23.4 (Patch 2020.1.1)

*Yay, though I walk through the valley of the shadow of
death, I will fear no evil, for thou art with me, the latest
Smartphone and Google Maps will comfort me, and lead
me along the path of self-righteousness and away from
real-world temptation.*

––––

As if modern city pavements weren't littered with enough
obstacles – lampposts, traffic signs, bike racks and
abandoned bicycles, litter bins, scooters, anti-terrorist
bollards – we now have 'phombies' who expect you to
take avoiding action, rather than be barged over by
them. But there is a solution, and it works:

STOP DEAD, in front of them, and their 'radar' will
identify you as an obstacle that they need to avoid.

––––––––––

After his wife's pacemaker fixed her heart murmur and re-energised her, Tony thought he should get one too, to catch up and resynchronise their previous rhythms.

———————

I like fresh flowers, but I also find that those past their best but with life still in them are equally attractive, much the same as women.

———————

Donald Trump isn't the problem, but the 60 million odd people who voted for him. And in the UK, it isn't the 'Pied Piper of Brexitannia', but the Conservative Party. They believed that with no compass, magnetic or moral, he was the best man to lead 15 million blind lemmings off the White Cliffs of Dover, and the country with them.

———

The UK democracy has descended into farce, in which an unelected government advisor leads a half-wit of a Prime Minister and his amoral flock into the wilderness.

———

I sent off for a cheap See Britain travel pass, and all the agent sent me was a Location Guide to UK Opticians, and a Dominic Cummings face mask.

———————

VIRUS UPDATE

Jesus: Have You tried switching it off and on again?

God: Look, I might be old but I'm not stupid. Of course I have, 65 million years ago, and look what happened...

———

TABULA RASA
2019
Dan Dare

screenshot

2020: THE YEAR THE WORLD FROZE IN FEAR

The absurd panic and over-reaction to the coronavirus is an embarrassment that has its modern-era origins in the 9/11 paranoia of 2001. That resulted in USA imposition of fascist airport security on the rest of the world.

COVIDIOTS

UK Secretary of State for Health, Matt Hancock:

"The government is 'absolutely confident' there will be no shortage of food or essential items."

Result: No toilet rolls and empty shelves everywhere…

LETTER TO FT

Open letter to: Rt Hon Matt Hancock, MP.
Secretary of State for Health and Social Care

Dear Minister

Despite your unfounded confidence in the ability of our supermarkets to maintain supplies during the pandemic panic, yesterday my local Waitrose ran out of their quite nice but rather expensive own brand, deluxe, mixed-fruit muesli.

Perhaps you could have a word with them.

Jack Idle

The first morning, I couldn't get a seat on the train, so I called the coronavirus hotline to make an appointment...

———

In my splendid isolation and eerie silence, I felt very regal, almost prime-ministerial, until I discovered that white suited figures had turned it into a ghost train.

———

I had to stop following the PM's coronavirus advice so literally, after I was inundated with birthday cards.

———

The White House confirmed that the President's virus test was so negative he is the only person on the planet clinically certified as immune to kryptonite.

———

LETTER TO FT

Sir

There are 8.76 million people in UK over the age of 70. Instead of strangling the country's economy in panic response to the coronavirus, to the tune of £350 billion and incalculably more, perhaps Messrs. Cummings, Johnson, Sunak and Co. should have bunged each and every one of them £30k to lavish on a bargain-basement round-the-world cruise to keep them out of harm's way. We would all have come out winners.

I've done the sums in my head, and it's a no-brainer...

Jack Idle

———

An Imperial College London team carried out some complex mathematical modelling and calculated that without draconian intervention by government, the virus death toll could be 550,000, almost as high as the annual average number of UK deaths of 600,000. Meanwhile, in a fag-packet exercise, based on toilet roll sales and a supermarket checkout poll, a UCL duo concluded that no such action was necessary, since total deaths would be kept to around 40,000, due to everyone's need to sit at home in regal isolation.

———————

STAY AT HOME. DIE AT HOME. PROTECT THE NHS.

So, he claimed national house-arrest was essential, to protect the NHS from being overwhelmed. But I thought the NHS was there to protect us – our health and lives.

———

And so it came to pass. The imposition of house-arrest swapped herd immunity with herd panic and stupidity, and an anal obsession with personal hygiene and total risk aversion.

———

ONYER BIKE, BORIS

The government has updated the old school game, 'Simon says', used to train children into obedience:

Boris says, 'Stay at home'. Boris says, 'Wash your hands'. Boris says, 'Back to work'…etc., etc.

The winners are the grown-ups who refuse to play.

———————

With his wife stuck overseas, the only recreation my friend Dan had was going along to the local store with his walking stick and torch, to look under the gondolas for anything edible or useful that had fallen on to the floor and rolled out of reach. All he found was a torn but usable wrapper off a toilet roll multi-pack, a mouldy tomato, half a banana, and a sticky cough pastille.

I said to him, "I didn't realise you were desperate, Dan."

I knew Dan wasn't as daring as his name suggested, so I wasn't too surprised that he always wore a face mask, even in bed. But with no forecast of heavy or even light rain, I thought the oxygen tank and flippers were a bit over the top.

THE VIRUS OF FEAR

I had an idle thought that the virus might be an alien diversion, to convince the whole world to stay at home, so they could invade us without our seeing them arrive, and be unable to stop them before it was too late.
So, for days during house-arrest, I would sit behind my front door, peering out of the letterbox through my home-made cardboard periscope, scanning the street for any signs of unusual activity or strange beings...

I ended up in A+E one morning after the postman punched me in the face with my mail. The next time I need some fresh air I'll open the door, and not just the letterbox.

It's telling that the government's choice of the word, *lockdown,* has its origins in the world of prisons. Should we infer from this, that this is now the government-electorate relationship that we are being conditioned to embrace, at no less than two-metres distance?

It looks set to become one of those annoying annual events, but unlike April Fool's Day, November 5th, Black Friday, or Halloween, this will have the freedom to pop up at random, as a mask for government incompetence, or another excuse for proroguing Parliament.

————

It's odd that nowhere in Europe has there been a single graph that shows lockdown's impact or effectiveness.

————————

Who knows how or where he caught the virus, but BJ's neural pathways have now found it impossible to identify when and which orifice he needs to open and close.

————————

A SIGNED LETTER FROM THE PRIME MINISTER

My heart lifted and sank again when I read his words:

"It's important for me to level with you – we know things will get worse before they get better."

Is he about to confess that he lied to us all, and that the £350 million a week was actually only £137 million?

But no, he has now fully recovered from the virus and will carry on misleading us into the wilderness.

————

LETTER TO FT

3rd May 2020

Sir

I was sceptical when I heard of BJ's miraculous three day Easter resurrection, and how he had avoided death with life-saving 'litres and litres of oxygen', but not I hope 350 million litres, or three days-worth for 50,000 other patients. We all need oxygen, Boris, usually about 2,000 litres every day, most of which is exhaled, unused and available for recycling, uncontaminated by dishonesty. But that aside, thanks to his forward thinking, my quota is now a home delivery through my letterbox.

Meanwhile, his Cabinet of yes-men has come up with a series of wheezes to convince a sceptical public that things are under control. These include PPE, temporary hospitals, cold-storage mortuaries to deal with the threatened overwhelming body count, post-infection testing, but only if you have actually got the virus or you are an 'essential worker', and finally, the economy. But not, it seems, how to extricate ourselves from the new 'fine mess he has got us into', without living with more deaths of the old and sick. They account for around 17% of the population, but less than one third of one percent may eventually succumb to the virus, principally because of their pre-existing serious health conditions.

If anyone thinks that I am heartlessly or unfairly playing down what has been oversold as a major threat, maybe the following graphic and data will disabuse them…

Jack Idle

———

THE SCALE OF THE UK COVID-19 THREAT

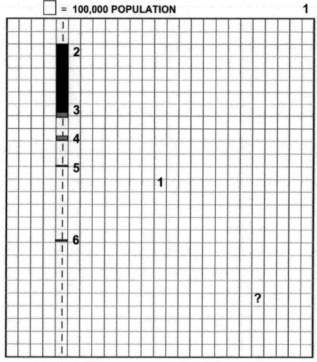

□ = 100,000 POPULATION   1

12,000,000 >|< 56,000,000
vulnerable   immune or mild symptoms and non-life threatening

<   67,800,000 = UK TOTAL POPULATION   >

AND THE AFTERMATH

1	67,800,000	**UK POPULATION (2019)**
2	620,000	**ANNUAL DEATHS - ALL CAUSES** (including respiratory deaths)
3	42,000	**RESPIRATORY DEATHS (2018)**
4	40,000	**COVID-19 DEATHS (estimated)**
5	5,000	**NET COVID-19 DEATHS (estimated)** (after subtraction of 87% of deaths with underlying serious or terminal illness)
6	20,000	**COLLATERAL DEATHS (estimated)** (caused by fear, neglect, oversight etc)
?	30,000,000	**MEDIUM & LONG-TERM SCARRED** (cultural, economic, mental, social etc) (unknown but assumed to be ~50% until hard data becomes available)

The worst aspect of the virus was the incompatibility of those terrifying tabloids and my haemorrhoids.

Cleverly, I installed an old printer in the lavatory, and had my friends email me some better newspapers.

————————

BBC BROKEN NEWS

At his Press Briefing, Health Secretary Matt Hancock bragged that there was enough PPE kit for everyone, and then unveiled his plan for addressing shortages. He then explained the apparent contradiction in his statement, that the kit was in a cupboard somewhere, but the man who had the key was now on a ventilator.

————————

A WHITEHALL FARCE

Act 1: Pinocchio stands on his soapbox and imposes house-arrest on the country, then he catches the virus himself and passes it on to his friends. After resurrection with litres and litres of oxygen, he sneaks off to his other home in the country and more litres and litres of oxygen.

Act 2: The dodgy Professor Doom reappears with his mickey-mouse abacus, and flouting his own codswallop advice is caught with his trousers down...

Act 3: Geppetto the puppeteer appears from the wings, cuts Pinocchio's braces, pulls his trousers down, jumps into his car and drives off with them, chased by the paparazzi. Meanwhile, Pinocchio, turning his back on his audience, bows and farts...

————————

GOINGS AND COMINGS

After months of being penned up alone with me, the wife announced she was leaving me, or as she referred to it, 'permanent long-range social-distancing'.

So, I've just spent a week in bed with a new friend, or as she likes to call it, in 'voluntary lockdown'.

Mysterious particles found in Antarctica are thought to be the first evidence of the theoretical Anti-Universe, where everything is the opposite of our own Universe.
But proof of this has already appeared in the new lockdown UK, where the normal rules of civilised behaviour have been blown away, to create a national asylum in which the sane are safely locked up, and the keys held by the lunatics.

THE KISS OF DEATH

With the word virus on everyone's lips, it's only a matter of time before they ban kissing…

OUT OF THE FRYING PAN…

At the end of house-arrest, I went out wearing my black ski balaclava, an *ad hoc* mandatory face mask, and was immediately arrested by the police.
I'm not sure if it was because they thought black people might be offended by my appearance, or because they thought I was black…

THE INSANITY OF ISOLATION

I heard that self-isolation has driven many people mad.

It was only yesterday that I was discussing this over a cup of tea and chocolate gingers with my kettle and teapot, when both of them spouted out that things weren't as serious as that mendacious, scaremongering charlatan would have us all believe.

Earlier on, the washing machine had been rumbling on that things might be spinning out of control, while the freezer, who had been quietly humming to itself, then spluttered into action, noting that everyone seemed to be getting rather overheated about it and needed to cool down. In the end, the steam iron reminded everyone that there were more pressing matters that needed straightening out, before the vacuum cleaner who had been quietly taking everything in, and the electric fan who had been swinging one way and then the other, both concluded it was a load of hot air that would soon blow over. My desk lamp had briefly beamed into action in a futile attempt to shed some light on all the figures, but soon gave up, leaving us all still largely in the dark.

Upstairs, the toilet seat was looking very depressed, and wanted to know why his visitors were ignoring the advice to maintain social-distancing, and suggested that like everyone else, he would benefit from a bit of fresh air. But when I drew the curtains back to open the window, my pyjamas, still relaxing on the bedroom floor, stirred, and complained they had only just persuaded them to pull themselves together, and that it was already past everyone's bedtime, again.

––––––––––––

THE PRICE OF AUTOCRACY

The lingerie retailer has gone bust.
The beauty parlour is facing an ugly downturn.
The newspaper stand has folded.
The builders' merchant has gone to the wall.
The juice bar has gone into liquidation.
The laundrette is washed up.
The bakery is now toast.
The funeral parlour is dead and buried.
The fish 'n' chip shop has taken a battering.
The sign maker is barely hanging on.
The wine bar is now scraping the barrel.
The barber has had to trim his staff.
The hardware shop is screwed.
The glazier's is boarded up.
The glove shop has changed hands.
The upholsterer looks unlikely to recover.
The blind shop has closed down.
The opticians see no future in the business.
The carpet seller had the rug pulled from under his feet.
The cab company has fared badly.
The watchmaker has wound up.
The florist's business has wilted.
The car battery and tyre business is flat.
The fitness centre has run into trouble.
The paving company has reached the end of the road.
The shipping company has packed up.
The pet shop has gone to the dogs with the rest of the
country, as the new regime takes control and its toll…

———

Sitting at home just one day a week, a whoopee cushion
would make a better job of running the country.

———————

LETTER TO FT

10th May 2020

Sir

In thinking about how to bring this fascist-imposed disaster to an end, quickly, painlessly and with certainty, I have considered most of the commonly tried and tested methods – an overdose, poison, lethal injection, stiletto through the heart, strangulation, etc.

Then today, we had BJ's vacuous pronouncement, revealing to all the addling effect the virus had on the logic pathways of his infected brain. And by inverting my own logic, it struck me there was a painless way out this mess – the vehicle-mounted rocket-launcher and SSM.

Demand is high, but if you can afford one, or better still a truck load, the Saab RBS15 Mk3, reliably guided by NERVTAG's new hot-air seeking 'track and trace' app, can be discretely delivered at a time-slot of your choice, from the back of any unmodified Ocado van.

Jack Idle

————

The UK government was instantly able to impose its national house-arrest, but inexplicably, unable to lift it as instantly, as it had with the 'all-clear' sirens in WW2. And in overriding WHO's advice on the sensible wearing of face masks and safe distancing, it only succeeded in perpetuating its 'climate of fear' in order to remind us of the menace that remained, and we had yet to face…

——

MAKE YOUR OWN ANTI-VIRUS FACE MASK

- Enlarge the image to A4 size to cover your face.
- Use your crayons to make the eyes more scary.
- Cut eye holes if you want to see ahead.
- Use a hole punch to cut side holes as shown.
- Insert elastic or string into the holes and secure.
- Fasten mask tightly around your head.
- Pray the virus will go away and leave you alone.

ANTI-SOCIAL-DISTANCING-MASK
2020
Dan Dare

lockdown maintenance tool

THE FINAL PUZZLE PAGE

JOIN THE DOTS
in their correct order of stellar magnitude to
reveal the mysterious being known as God.

Eventually the human race will wipe itself out in another fearful pandemic – the fear of inappropriate touching.

————

I guess living life in a protective bubble is like dying slowly in an extra-large condom.

————————

Despite my film-star qualities, you wouldn't catch me talking to a woman without a written invitation, in case it was interpreted as flirting. And as for flirting, I'm sure suicide is the least painful alternative.

————

I saw a news report about the death of a 70-year-old man who was being privately entertained by a brace of glamorous beauties, a birthday-treat arranged by his brother, after which the coroner had returned a verdict of 'death by natural causes'.

I have stopped drinking, smoking and driving recklessly, and for anyone interested, my birthday is on 20th July.

(Further details from my publisher ;)

————

I was hoping to live until I reach a hundred, not because I'll get a text message from the King by then, but because very few people die after that age.

————

But as a time-traveller, I then realised age is irrelevant. I could go anywhere and everywhere, past, present, and future, forever and ever, just like God, if there is one…

————

IS THERE A GOD?

According to eccentric British artist, John Latham:

> THE MYSTERIOUS BEING KNOWN AS GOD
> is an atemporal score, with a probable
> **time-base** in the region of 10^{19} seconds.

That may look and sound like a small number, but it works out to be about twenty-three times the current age of the Universe, when according to some cosmologists, everything in the Universe will finally cease to emit any heat or light, and everything is dead, perhaps God too, and even Hell freezes over.

It was my unanswered prayers that made me realise that if I am talking to myself, I might actually be God.

If I am wrong and I do meet Him, I'm going to ask Him why the hell He never answered any of my calls for help, and suggest that He gets up to date and installs a proper answering service, and with real people on it.

Anyway, in view of the fate of the planet in a little over a billion years from now, I am postponing my second coming, and plan to return as a phoenix.

But before I go, here is a message from our sponsors:

Behave yourself or go to Hell.

JACK OUT OF THE BOX

St Peter: Didn't you try to sneak in here a couple of years ago after you Scousers stole our gates?

Jack: No, that wasn't me, and anyway, I'm better now.

THE JACKPOT QUESTION

St Peter: Okay, Jack, you only scraped through the previous rounds, so take your time with this one:

"Are you anti-Semitic?"

Jack: Well, without wishing to be pedantic, or semantic, I would say that in the same way that homosexuals have hijacked the word 'gay' for their exclusive self-referential use, and a code for their private activities, which denies me my use of the word to describe my rare state of happiness, without misleading people that I am anything other than a full-blooded, even rampant heterosexual male, it seems to me that Jews have done the same to their Arab brethren, by unilaterally denying them their historic inclusion in the broader definition of the term, 'Semite'. But, as a vehement and non-violent opponent of the Zionist State of Israel and its genocidal treatment of the Palestinian people, fellow Semites whose historic homelands they have brutally invaded and stolen with the active and amoral connivance of the world at large, I am also an equally vehement and passive supporter of Palestinian rights to justice, and so I would say,

"No, I am not anti-Semitic."

A BRIEF AUDIENCE WITH GOD

God: Greetings, Jack, well done, you passed the final test, and after a short quarantine, welcome to Heaven. Please make sure your device is in flight mode, selfies are strictly forbidden, and, contrary to the stories downstairs, no communication is permitted beyond the grave. There are more rules, but that'll do for starters. By the way, I'm God, but you can call me 'Sir'.

Jack: Yessir, but do you mind if I ask why You never answered my prayers nor anyone else's. I mean, if You have a high volume of calls at the same time, why don't You record them, so that You can deal with them later...

God: Look, I work in mysterious ways, and I get a ton of nuisance calls every day, mostly phishing for favours from people who don't really believe in me. Anyway, any more of this nonsense, and I'll send you down to the basement with the Jehovah's Witnesses and Zionists, the traffic engineers, and the other fascists and idiots.

Which reminds me, if Jesus asks for your ID, don't let it out of your sight. One of his really stupid tricks is to palm it for someone else's, to confuse you, and to annoy me.

And one last bit of advice, since the advent of the mobile phone and the plummeting standards of behaviour downstairs, I'm raising the bar up here next week, and all new arrivals will have to disable their phones or hand them in, or they'll be sent down to the basement as well.

Jack: Well, Sir, I'm on the same hymn sheet with You on that one, but right now, where is the bar?

––––––––––––

FREE THINKING

What if death were you abandoning your body, releasing your mind to roam the Universe and beyond?

Now, that really would be *'thinking outside the box'*.

THE END

…or the start of a new chapter?

EPILOGUE

Feedback is mostly a pointless exercise, but you might feel better if you give it a go:

1: How was your journey today?
You need to try harder, and every day.

2: Did our service meet your expectations?
It was very hit and miss and ran into trouble.

3: Did you get to your destination?
No, and I was one of the lucky ones.

4: Did you end your journey early, on time or late?
Early and late due to an unexplained breakdown.

5: Was your journey comfortable?
It was overcrowded with too many awful people.

6: Did you encounter any issues or problems?
So many I could fill a library of books with them.

7: How well did our staff respond to the problems?
With large helpings of platitudes for the hapless and helpless multitudes.

8: How could we have improved your experience?
Well for starters, when You accidentally wiped out the dinosaurs 65 million years ago, You should have resurrected them, because despite their intimidating size children adore them.
And, if You think this is Heaven, I'm sorry but You are living in cloud-cuckoo-land…

———————

ACKNOWLEDGEMENTS

I thank the following for their various contributions and inspiration, and their assistance in periodically inflating my enthusiasm and deflating my ego:

Thomas Aquinas
Robert Armstrong
Alan Bleasdale
Stoker Cavendish
Joel and Ethan Coen
Matt D'Arcy
Dan Dare
Paul Dirac
Edward Durkin
Yuval N Harari
Mel Hare
Harry Harrison
Tony Harrison
Ron Haslam
Mrs Hudson
Barbara Kruger
Simon Kuper
John Latham
Nadine Lockyer
Rosemarie McGurk
Red Molotov
Vera Mrdak
Douglas Murphy
George Orwell
Katie Paterson
Robert Shrimsley
Winston Smith
Jack Ware
Oscar Wilde

AN IDLE UNDERSTUDY
2004
Dan Dare

prototype 4D CGI EEG MR HoloLens video still

146

ABOUT THE AUTHOR

Jack Idle would often claim he landed on Earth in 1946 and spent his formative years as an inventor, his euphemism for making up stuff as excuses for not handing in his homework. However, there is mounting evidence that he first landed 500 years earlier, and teamed up with his fellow time-traveller and genius, Leonardo da Vinci, with whom he anonymously shared some of his own clever stuff, and provided draughting lessons, before moving on to do some ghost writing for William Shakespeare, and inspiring many of his fictional characters, especially Bottom and Falstaff.

His recent life remains a mystery, like the empty highlands of Iceland or the void of intergalactic space, both of which he disappears into from time to time, and from which he always returns with a new theory, or an invention such as his ultra-revolutionary, time-reversal washing machine, or one of his many annoying letters to various authorities or newspapers, most of which go unread, or ignored until it is too late.

In 2018, he emerged from a period of inactivity in some alien landscape, with the first opus magnum under his own name, *Idle Thoughts & Other Stuff*, followed by *Second Thoughts on My Way to the Crematorium,* before rounding off the trinity with this collection of final thoughts and other pearls of wisdom.

Upon its completion, he climbed back into his box, and as he closed the lid and disappeared into the future, his muffled parting words were,

"I'll be back…"

IN MEMORIAM

Following his character assassination and sudden disappearance after racing to the summit of the #MeToo hit list, in celebration of his legendary enthusiasm and fearless indifference in the face of rampant misandry, and his martyrdom in the renaissance of Masculine Activism, Jack Idle has posthumously awarded himself the CBA.

———————